Finding Freedom

FINDING FREEDOM

How Death Row Broke
and Opened My Heart

• • •

Jarvis Jay Masters

Foreword by Pema Chödrön

SHAMBHALA

Shambhala Publications, Inc.
4720 Walnut Street
Boulder, Colorado 80301
www.shambhala.com

Cover art: Moopsi / T30 Gallery / Shutterstock
Cover design: Daniel Urban-Brown
Interior design: Lora Zorian

9 8 7 6 5 4 3 2 1

Printed in the United States of America

∞ This edition is printed on acid-free paper that meets the
American National Standards Institute Z39.48 Standard.
♻ This book is printed on 30% postconsumer recycled paper.
For more information please visit www.shambhala.com.
Shambhala Publications is distributed worldwide by Penguin
Random House, Inc., and its subsidiaries.

See page 150 for a continuation of the copyright page

To my mother Cynthia, my sister Charlene, and my brother Tommy, who have all passed away during my years on San Quentin's death row—and to all sentient beings. May they find freedom.

Contents

Foreword

by Pema Chödrön

My dear friend, Jarvis Jay Masters, has been one of my greatest teachers.

This courageous man had a very painful early life. At the age of five, he entered the foster-care system, having first experienced hunger, neglect, and violence. He witnessed suffering and trauma at such an impressionable age, and, like too many who don't get the care and supportive environments they need in their young adulthood, he committed armed robbery and in his late teens ended up in San Quentin Prison.

While still serving his sentence in San Quentin, Jarvis was accused of conspiring to murder a prison guard. To this day, he maintains his innocence of that crime, and I've joined in the Free Jarvis campaign because I believe him. In the many years I've known Jarvis and visited him at San Quentin prison, I can see that he's undergone a profound personal transformation— one that has been a result of his own willingness to examine his heart and mind. On death row—where there is so much despair, anger, and hopelessness—Jarvis has emerged as a gentle man, one who has broken through the pain to find the tender humanity in his environment. In the Buddhist teachings, we call this compassion.

When you practice developing compassion as Jarvis has, you begin to see the world and your place in it from a much wider viewpoint. You learn to touch in and experience the truth that we are all fragile, vulnerable, and longing to be loved. Under the guidance of his first Buddhist teacher, Chagdud Tulku

Rinpoche, Jarvis took the bodhisattva vow, which essentially means devoting your life to compassion. In taking the vow, Jarvis committed to not hurt or harm any beings—and to do what he could to end suffering wherever he could. In his writings, his meditation practice, and his very presence, Jarvis sets that example for others every day. He gets letters all the time, especially from young people who are struggling as he did, who have heard his story and therefore turned their lives around.

I am continually inspired by Jarvis because of his steadfastness and resilience. I know it's not easy for him to sit with intense visible suffering on a daily basis knowing the situation might never change. And yet, Jarvis has found within himself the ability to be present to his experience, to accept, to open, to receive the lessons of his situation, and to keep his sense of humor. I often think to myself, if Jarvis can break through and find the light in this darkest of places, there's hope for all of us.

This is one of my favorite books, which I have often referred to in my teachings. I am delighted that it will have a wider publication now so that more people can read these wonderful heartfelt stories.

Preface

This book contains true stories of my experiences in San Quentin. Many of the names were changed to protect those still in prison, but the characters are all people I've known. That I write of their human side, not just their violent, hardened, humorless side, was a challenge for them. But they all welcomed it, and I've appreciated their willingness to embrace and support my writing.

The italicized portions of the book were compiled from my letters to friends over my years in San Quentin, as well as from notes they sometimes took during visits. I want to thank them for their permission to use this material. I've kept parts of letters written to friends to help me discover, understand, sit with so many changes going on in me. I hope they will help the reader understand the transitions I have undergone.

ACKNOWLEDGMENTS

My correspondents have been my companions, quiet listeners through whom I could hear myself speak, see the better part of myself reflected, and learn more about myself and the world around me. Their correspondence also helped me through troubled times. I want to thank them all, but especially Jim Cronin, Sarah Jane Freymann, Donna Gans, Pam Gerwe, Jane Hamilton, Kelly Hayden, Lisa Leghorn, Sarah Paris, Karen Poverny, Will Shonbrun, Diane Solomon, and Lynn Weinberger.

This book was born out of a process of self-discovery that I shared with Melody Ermachild Chavis, without whose belief in me, support, and encouragement for my case, my life, and my writing I wouldn't be who I am today. She guided me through the many steps from extreme anger to the clarity of my Buddhist practice. She created a bridge for me to the outside world, bringing people into my life and giving passage to my voice.

There are many I want to thank for their true and stable friendship and for their humor. They have loved me through my anger and have always held me as a part of their family, especially my loving sister Carlette, Betsy Doubobsky, Melody Ermachild Chavis, Donna Gans, Kelly Hayden, Elershey Johnson, and Conny Lindley. I am especially indebted to Lisa Leghorn, who worked with me diligently in creating this book. She helped me see its benefit and encouraged me, not only by her belief in me, but by her pushy, stubborn, loving, and determined insistence, telling me to "write, write, write." She is a person whose love has extended the radiant image of Tara to my heart. In my life, they are equal.

In particular, I want to thank Susan Moon from *Turning Wheel* for publishing my first stories; Linda Baer, Michael Bradfute, Mary Racine, and Anna Smith at Padma Publishing for their help with editing and production; Robert Racine of Padma Publishing and Kim McLaughlin of Chagdud Gonpa for their support of this project; Anna Smith and all the other typists and transcriptionists without whom this book could not have been produced from inside the walls of San Quentin; and Sarah Jane Freymann for her love, care, determination, and conviction as my agent in guiding me through the publication of this book.

Finally, without my precious teacher, Chagdud Tulku Rinpoche, I would not have my belief in the Buddhist path or know the true purpose of these words: benefiting others.

Introduction

by Melody Ermachild Chavis

As one of the defense investigators who prepared Jarvis's trial, I looked into the details of his life and learned how far he has traveled spiritually in one short lifetime. Jarvis was born in 1962, the same year my oldest child was born. I met Jarvis's mother, Cynthia, while working on his case, but she died of heart failure just before his trial. She had not seen him for many years. All of Cynthia's children were raised in foster care because she was addicted to drugs. Jarvis's father had left the family and later he too became an addict. In a series of foster care placements, Jarvis was separated from his siblings. For several years, he stayed in his favorite home, with an elderly couple he loved, but when they became too old to care for him, he was moved again, at the age of nine. After that, Jarvis ran away from several foster homes, and went back to the elderly people's house. He was then sent to the county's large locked facility for dependent children, and later to some more group homes. Once, he stayed with an aunt for a while, but he got in trouble. At twelve, he became a ward of the court because of delinquency, and was in and out of institutions after that.

During my investigation I met people who had known Jarvis in foster care and institutions, and they told me he had always had a lot of potential. They remembered a smart and articulate youngster with a sense of humor. But too many times he was pushed—and he went—in the wrong direction.

At the age of seventeen, when he was a very angry young man, he was released from the California Youth Authority and went on a crime spree, holding up stores and restaurants until he was captured and sent to San Quentin. He never shot anyone, but the big stack of reports that I read about his crimes was scary. As I told him, I'm glad I wasn't in Taco Bell when he came through.

When Jarvis arrived in San Quentin in 1981 he was nineteen. Right away he got involved in what the prison system calls a gang. Most young men coming into prison—black, brown, and white—group together for a sense of belonging, for family. In those days, older African American prisoners passed on political education to younger ones.

In 1985, an officer named Sergeant Burchfield was murdered in San Quentin, stabbed to death at night on the second tier of a cell block. At the time, Jarvis was locked in his cell on the fourth tier.

Although many inmates were suspected of conspiring to murder Sergeant Burchfield, only three were tried, Jarvis among them. One was accused of being the "spear man"—of actually stabbing the sergeant. Another, an older man, was accused of ordering the killing. Jarvis was accused of sharpening a piece of metal which was allegedly passed along and later used to make the spear with which the sergeant was stabbed.

In one of the longest trials in California history, all three were convicted of their parts in the conspiracy to kill Sergeant Burchfield. But their sentences varied. One jury gave the young spear man the death penalty, but the trial judge changed his sentence to life without parole because of his youth. Another jury could not reach a verdict on the older man's sentence, and so he was also given life without parole. Jarvis was sentenced by that same jury to death in the gas chamber, partly because of his violent background.

Although his lawyers asked the trial judge for leniency, also on the basis of his youth—he was twenty-three when the crime occurred, just two years older than the accused spear man—she denied this appeal and sent him to death row. He has been there since 1990. There he must be patient, waiting for appeals to be filed, waiting for the outcomes.

Jarvis's situation is unique in one way: he is the only man on death row living in his crime scene. It's as if he'd been convicted of killing a store clerk in a robbery, and his cell had been set up in that same store, so that for the rest of his life, his every move was watched and he was even fed by people who identified with his victim, people who thought every day about the dead clerk's wife and children. And some day, several of the workers at that store might participate in executing Jarvis. Jarvis has more opportunity than most people on this earth to face up to how people feel about him.

Jarvis is usually stoic about his situation. He talks about karma, and the path he himself took, the choices he made. He often asks me to tell the "at-risk" youths I volunteer with, "You guys still have choices!"

The hardest thing is that he has so few. He doesn't live on ordinary death row. Because the crime he is convicted of involved a guard, he lives in San Quentin's security housing unit called the Adjustment Center. Men on the more relaxed part of death row can make phone calls, listen to tapes, use typewriters. Those in the security housing can have only a few books and a TV. They stay in their cells for all but a few hours of yard time three times each week. Jarvis cannot choose what or when to eat, when to exercise or shower. He can't turn the tier lights off or on, regulate the temperature in his cell, or have any control over when he receives visits or how long they last. I think it must be almost impossible to grow into a mature, responsible man when one is infantilized this way, and yet I have seen Jarvis grow.

Jarvis is very different today from the troubled defensive

young man I met in 1986. He even looks different. When I met him, his face had a sullen, callous expression. But, as happens so often to patients with fatal or life-threatening illnesses, facing his death has opened him up. Having arrived at San Quentin with minimal reading and writing skills, he began to educate himself and to meditate. As I write, he is a mature thirty-five-year-old man, and he plays a constructive role on death row, helping younger men.

Not all officers hold a grudge against Jarvis. Quite a few have told me they respect the changes he has made in himself. I can tell from the relaxed bodies of the officers who know him that they do not fear him. In contrast to how they handle some other clients of mine, many greet Jarvis, smile at him, touch his shoulder. When I arrive for a visit, typically several officers I run into on my way in tell me to say hi to him.

Sergeant Burchfield was killed in June, and if Jarvis is going to have trouble with staff in the prison, it sometimes comes in the month of June. A few times during this month, Jarvis has been placed in the worst part of the prison—on the bottom tier of the security housing. The authorities who make this decision explain it as a "convenience." This move is usually stressful at first, because Jarvis's belongings—including his personal books and legal papers—are all taken from him, although they are later returned.

On that bottom tier of the security housing is a row of cells where the most problematic prisoners are kept. There, Jarvis's neighbors yell all day and all night, and some have hallucinations in which insects are crawling on their bodies or other people are in their cells. Some do not clean themselves or refuse to eat for fear of being poisoned. If inmates in this condition don't improve, they are eventually sent to hospital prisons and officially designated mentally ill. But in the meantime, they can be segregated, as they are in the security housing.

During those hard months Jarvis spends on the bottom tier, it is particularly difficult for me to watch him get ready to go back to his cell after our visits, which are among the few pleasant times he has. Ordinarily, Jarvis smiles and says goodbye, holding his hands behind him, close to the portal in the metal door so that the officer can reach through and ratchet cuffs onto his wrists. But when he's living on this tier, when the time is up, he doesn't smile. I don't know what else to do, except stand patiently an extra second holding my papers, waiting for him to go.

During those months, I worry more about him than I usually do, afraid he will get sick or depressed. But he keeps up his spirits amazingly well. He says that in a way his new neighbors are easy to live with, because no matter what they do, he can't really get mad at them.

Currently, Jarvis is living back upstairs in a warmer, drier cell. The men on either side are very quiet, giving him the best meditating and writing conditions he has had at San Quentin. Across from his cell is a window. Jarvis is glad the glass is broken, because although the air is cold sometimes, it's fresh. Best of all, through the window Jarvis can see some far-off houses. Several children play outside, riding tricycles and throwing balls. Jarvis has given the children names, and he's gotten to know them individually by watching them for hours as they play. At Christmas time, he can see the homes decorated with colored lights, the first he's seen for many years.

Jarvis has been in prison so long, he loves to hear about the details of ordinary life. (I tease him that he probably went to jail before airplanes were invented. It's true he's never flown in one.) So I describe the pungent, crowded atmosphere of a favorite cafe, the students with their laptops, the smell of espresso, the stacks of free weekly papers.

Jarvis wants to know all about a hike or a family dinner, how it looked, felt, tasted, all the flavor of life that's missing inside. When I tell such stories, we're not exactly living in the moment. In fact, we're not present in San Quentin at all. He is leaning back, smiling, imagining himself with my family or friends. I am reliving some recent event my own life, seeing it all again. From Jarvis's perspective my life is so rich, so complex, the world so beautiful.

I usually write *with* Jarvis, not about him. When we write together at the prison, we take a break from discussing the appeal of his case. I take off my watch and put it where he can see it on the ledge between us and one of us says, "All right, ten minutes, OK? Go!" The idea of this exercise is to loosen up our writer's muscles without worrying about results. We just write, sometimes about a particular topic, such as "A Conversation Overheard" or "Rain." Sometimes we write whatever comes, just keeping our pens moving. He on his side of the thick wire mesh, and I on my side, the side with the door to the outside world—we both of us put our heads down and scribble away. We are breathing the same stale prison air. We can both hear the murmur of other visits through the walls, and occasionally a guard's voice calling out. Jarvis has more light—the visitor's side of the visiting booth is dim and the prisoner's side is brightly lit with a fluorescent tube.

I have an ordinary ballpoint pen, but he has only the innards of one; he's not allowed to have the hard plastic case, so he writes with the flimsy plastic tube of ink. We are both equally intent on getting words onto paper. When our writing time is over, Jarvis and I read the results to each other. These brief shared writing exercises encourage both of us to keep on writing, and sometimes together we produce seeds that later grow into Jarvis's stories and my essays.

His writing and his meditation practice are what make life worth living for Jarvis. Studying Buddhism these past few years has helped him to gain remarkable insight. Neither he nor I have any illusions about the fact that he has harmed others. But he has taken the precepts of dedicating his remaining life to compassion and nonviolence—not an easy path in a violent prison.

There are many constraints on what Jarvis can write about, many of which can easily be imagined by any reader, as well as others that might be apparent only to those working or living within the penal system. And because his appeals are pending, Jarvis cannot write about his case. His appeals will go to both the state and federal courts, and he will not be close to execution or freedom for at least two more years.

Jarvis hopes, as he has written, that "those who want to try to make sense of it will see, through my writing, a human being who made mistakes. Maybe my writing will at least help them see me as someone who felt, loved, and cared, someone who wanted to know for himself who he was."

Some readers may find themselves eager for more details about Jarvis's life and transformation. It is my hope and fervent prayer that the conditions of Jarvis's life will change so that those stories may be written.

SANCTUARY

SANCTUARY

When I first entered the gates of San Quentin in the winter of 1981, I walked across the upper yard holding a box called a "fish-kit" filled with my prison-issued belongings. I saw the faces of hundreds who had already made the prison their home. I watched them stare at me with piercing eyes, their faces rugged and their beards of different shades—all dressed in prison blue jeans and worn, torn coats—some leaning against the chain fences, cigarettes hanging from their lips, others with dark glasses covering their eyes.

I will never forget when the steel cell door slammed shut behind me. I stood in the darkness trying to fix my eyes and readjust the thoughts that were telling me that this was not home—that this tiny space would not, could not be where I would spend more than a decade of my life. My mind kept saying, "No! Hell no!" I thought again of the many prisoners I had seen moments ago standing on the yard, so old and accustomed to their fates.

I dropped my fish-kit. I spread my arms and found that the palms of my hands touched the walls with ease. I pushed against them with all my might, until I realized how silly it was to think that these thick concrete walls would somehow budge. I groped for the light switch. It was on the back wall, only a few feet above the steel-plated bunk bed. The bed was bolted into the wall like a shelf. It was only two and a half feet wide by six feet long, and only several feet above the gray concrete floor.

My eyes had adjusted to the darkness by the time I turned the lights on. But until now I hadn't seen the swarms of cockroaches clustered about, especially around the combined toilet and sink on the back wall. When the light came on, the roaches scattered, dashing into tiny holes and cracks behind the sink and in the walls, leaving only the very fat and young ones still running scared. I was beyond shock to see so many of these nasty creatures. And although they didn't come near me, I began to feel roaches climbing all over my body. I even imagined them mounting an attack on me when I was asleep.

This was home. For hours I couldn't bear the thought. The roaches, the filth plastered on the walls, the dirt balls collecting on the floor, and the awful smell of urine left in the toilet for God knows how long sickened me nearly to the point of passing out.

To find home in San Quentin I had to summon an unbelievable will to survive. My first step was to flush the toilet. To my surprise I found all I needed to clean my cell in the fish-kit—a towel, face cloth, and a box of state detergent. There were also a bar of state soap, a toothbrush and comb, a small can of powdered toothpaste, a small plastic cup, and two twenty-year-old *National Geographic* magazines, one of them from the month and year of my birth.

It seemed that time was now on my side. I started cleaning vigorously. I began with one wall, then went on to the next, scrubbing them from top to bottom as hard as I could to remove the markings and filth. I didn't stop until I had washed them down to the floor and they were spotless. If I had to sleep in here, this was the least I could do. The cell bars, sink and toilet, and floor got the same treatment. I was especially worried about the toilet. I had heard that prisoners were compelled to wash their faces in their toilets whenever tear gas was shot into the units to break up mass disruptions and the water was turned off. I imagined leaning into this toilet, and I cleaned it to the highest military standards.

I spent hours, sometimes on my hands and knees, washing down every inch of my cell—even the ceiling. When I had finished, I was convinced that I could eat a piece of candy that had dropped onto the floor. The roaches had all drowned or been killed. I blocked off all their hiding places by plugging up the holes and cracks in the walls with wet toilet paper.

After the first days had passed, I decided to decorate my walls with photographs from the *National Geographic* magazines. The landscapes of Malaysia and other parts of the world had enormous beauty, and I gladly pasted photos of them everywhere. These small representations of life helped me to imagine the world beyond prison walls.

Over the years, I collected books and even acquired a television and radio—windows to the outside world. And I pasted many thousands of photographs on the wall. The one that has made my prison home most like a sanctuary to me is a small photograph of a Buddhist saint that a very dear friend sent to me. It has been in the center of my wall for a number of years.

I now begin every day with the practice of meditation, seated on the cold morning floor, cushioned only by my neatly folded blanket. Welcoming the morning light, I realize, like seeing through clouds, that home is wherever the heart can be found.

RATS

I was a fish, a new convict at San Quentin, sitting alone on my bunk, looking around on that first morning. An older, haunted-looking con, maybe in his late forties, came up to my cell, puffing on a cigarette butt.

"Hey," he said to me, "you seen anybody run by your cell?"

"No, I just got here last night."

"Oh, is that right? They call me Pops in these parts. Son, how old are you?"

I stood up. "Nineteen. I be twenty next month, though."

"So you're only nineteen, huh? You sure you haven't seen anything run by this morning?"

"No. What's up?" I asked.

"King done ran off without me."

"Who's King?"

"My pet rat. He's running around here someplace. He broke loose this morning."

"Rat! I haven't seen any rats."

"Well, King is very noticeable. He comes up to about your ankle. Black and real fat. Pretty, too." He smiled, trying to take a puff without burning his lips on the rolly butt. "Son, if you see King, he should have a fine string leash around his neck."

"Shit! You say he comes up to my ankle?"

"Yeah, maybe a little bigger. Give me a holler if you see him. Don't try to handle him, because he'll getcha."

"OK, Pops."

I sat back down, then snatched my feet onto my bunk.

LITTLE BLACK SPARROW

It was my first day out on the prison exercise yard. I had been in San Quentin for only a week and was going through the orientation of a new con—a sort of new walking number. Not knowing anyone, I stood nervously alone that early morning.

With my back against the prison fence, I gazed out across the yard at what seemed to be hundreds of prisoners—some strolling, some conversing, others lifting weights, playing handball, or sitting at the game tables, playing cards and dominoes.

The game tables were closest to me. Seated around them were all the older cons—shucking and jiving, slamming cards down on the table in rapid motion. It was exciting to see these older statesmen of San Quentin, with their gray hair and beards, drinking cold coffee like vintage wine, cigarettes hanging from their lips.

They played in an almost taunting way—challenging each other with intimidation and a kind of wisdom in anticipating their opponent's next play.

"Yeah, uh! I got your rabbit-ass now," one of them would say, taking a card from his hand, slamming it as hard as he could on the table.

"Ah, man—that ain't shit! That jack of diamonds can't cut you paper in a wood factory," the next con would shout, throwing down a queen of hearts. "Now you beat that wit' yo' bad ass. Y'all didn't think old Satchmo had her, huh? Let me tell y'all somethin'—I'm married to her. I'm the one with the big nuts around this table," he would boast, jaw-jacking in harmony with everyone around the table.

I drew closer. They reminded me of all the winos I had known as a child from the old neighborhood pool hall near my aunt's house. The only difference was that these men were hanging out in a prison yard.

When the card game came to an end, it was midday. By then Satchmo, who had been making me laugh with his wisecracks, stood up proudly from the table with a cigarette stub hanging from the corner of his mouth. He grinned.

"What's up, youngster? Now you see who the king is in this neck of the woods when it comes to playin' cards. These old dudes, look at 'em, they can't fuck with no youngsters like us."

"What do you mean, 'us'?" said Ripsaw. "Man, Satchmo, don't you be lyin' to that young'un. You older than all this penitentiary asphalt out here, so don't you be tellin' that stuff 'bout we bein' old—you jes' as old as us."

"He knows it," said Shorty, another old card player. He turned and smiled. "Youngster, that man is not your age! He ain't been your age since the early sixties, so don't you believe him. Come soon, he'll be sixty-two."

"Man, you must be out yo' cotton-pickin' mind," Satchmo burst out, as we broke into laughter. "Shit, I'm only forty-eight and won't be forty-nine until way, way, way next year."

"Man, is that right?" I said. "Wow! I figured you to be more like thirty-two. You don't look much older than that, Satchmo, seriously!"

"Yeah, that's right," he said with a huge Kool-Aid grin. "They don't know what the hell they be talkin' 'bout. Let's take a walk around the yard. I like your style. You want a cigarette? You's all right, youngster. All these old dudes, look at 'em, they bad, so bad on the spirit. Come on, let's get away from these ol' dinosaurs."

We spoke at length as we strolled slowly around the exercise yard. I was only nineteen. After Satchmo told me he'd been in San Quentin for sixteen years, I started to pay more attention.

"Youngster, let me tell you something," he said. "I can point out every nook and cranny about this penitentiary, from who's who to what's under the earth, you dig? But since that would take me years—and I don't know you too well—let me just tell you a little story that was passed on to me and others when we first arrived here. It's about a northern sparrow named Young Black, who hated to fly south for the winter."

It was an old story, but in my present circumstances it took on new meaning.

"Young Black hated the thought of leaving his nest home so much that he put off his journey until the last possible moment. After saying goodbye to all his friends flying south, he stayed in his nest five months against the laws of nature. Then the weather turned bitter cold and he couldn't delay his flight any longer. So Young Black started to fly south. Soon it began to snow, and ice formed on his little wings.

"Almost dead from cold and exhaustion, he fell to the ground and landed in a barnyard—we'll just call this barnyard San Quentin," Satchmo said, looking at me.

"Now, as the young sparrow was breathing what he thought might be his final breath, a brown horse walked out of the barn and moved his bowels, covering Young Black with hot, steaming fertilizer. At first, Young Black got extremely upset, twitting, 'You ass! What in the hell are you doing?' This was surely a hot and shitty way to die.

"But after a while, the hot fertilizer warmed his frozen feathers, and life returned to his body. To his surprise, he discovered he could breathe. Young Black began to chirp so loud that his song could be heard for miles around the yard.

"Then, slowly, a big white cat named Bobcat came creeping

toward the little singing jailbird. OP Bobcat dug into the pile of fertilizer and found where the singing was coming from. It took him a while, but in the end he caught Young Black and ate him."

"Damn!" I said. "I can't believe the cat just ate Young Black like that! Man, that's pretty cold-blooded, isn't it?"

"Not if you righteously think about it," Satchmo replied. "You see, young'un, there are some lessons to this. First, not everybody who shits on you is your enemy. Second, not everybody who takes shit off you is your friend. And finally, young'un," Satchmo paused and stared across the yard, "if you ever get warm and comfortable out there, even if it's in a pile of shit, you keep your mouth shut!"

PABLO'S WISH

I knew something wasn't right when I left my cell that morning to go to the yard. It was nothing more than a feeling, a convict's instinct, perhaps, as I observed the strange maneuvering of some other prisoners also making their way down to the lower yard for three hours of exercise time.

I had been in San Quentin less than two years, but by then I had seen more than enough to realize as I passed through the lower yard gate that a hit was going to come down. Someone was going to be stabbed.

It was no business of mine. I went about the yard, taking in some air before getting into my daily routine of playing a few games of dominoes and then jogging several laps around the yard.

While jogging, I spotted an old familiar face and smiled in a "misery loves company" kind of way. I hadn't seen Pablo since the early spring of 1972. In those days we had both been juvenile delinquents who always showed up in the same corridors of Juvenile Hall. We liked it there, we'd once joked.

"Damn, Pablo! Is that you? Where have you been, dude?" I asked, elated to see my old road dog and friend squatting down against the south block wall, puffing on a cigarette. I could tell that he had just arrived at San Quentin and didn't know his way around the exercise yard. He seemed nervous.

"Hey, Jarvis!" said Pablo, with obvious surprise. "How you been doing? Shit, man, I haven't seen you in ages. I thought you were dead. How long has it been—ten, fifteen years?"

"Yeah, it's been about that long." I smiled. "Man, I been here almost two years now. But what about you? Where have you been? The last time I seen you, we were both in juvenile detention for stealing a pack of cigarettes. You remember that?"

"Yeah, I remember," Pablo said, grinning. "We crawled out of the dormitory that one night and got caught trying to steal a pack of Camels out of the counselor's shirt when we thought he was sleeping." Pablo laughed. "Man, since then, I've been all through this rat-hole system. I did a little county camp time after I seen you. Then I did a few years in the California Youth Authority. I hit the big time after that—man, straight to the penitentiary. This is my fourth time in the joint. Plus, I did five years for the Feds in Lompoc!"

"How much time do you have now?"

Pablo was silent. The cigarette in his mouth began to puff like a hot chimney. His face twitched with fear. Then with his eyes fixed on the prison yard, he answered, "Well, Jarvis, I estimate two hours, tops."

"Damn, Pablo. What's going on?" I asked. I had only to look at his eyes to see that I had been right about the hit, and that Pablo was the marked man.

Pablo lit another cigarette. "Man, it's a long story," he said, exhaling. "All I can tell you is that I really fucked up this time. I've gotten into somethin' I can't get out of, and I know they'll be comin' for my head before I leave this yard. So it's best that you don't know."

"What can I do to help?"

"Man, there isn't really nothin' you can do. Just reach into my coat pocket," he said, trying to hide even from me the weapon slipped up his sleeve. "There's an envelope with an address and a photograph of my little girl Alice inside. She's my heart. If anything happens to me today, Jay, do me this favor and write to her. Tell her that I love her. Tell her something sweet for me."

"Ah, man! You know I'll do that for you. But what can I do now? Pablo—talk to me. Check: I'm willing to stand here and go down with you."

"No!" said Pablo. "Jay, this is *not* your fight. We'll both die, man, if you hang around much longer. This is some real serious shit I'm caught in, and if it goes down, I want to be by myself. Don't worry about me—I'm goin' down with a fight. And they know it."

I didn't know what to say. Pablo held out his hand and began laughing as we shook. "Man," he said, "I sure wish we could've ran into each other without all this other shit happenin'. We must have a million things we could talk about, huh? But now isn't the time. I'm serious, Jarvis. You have to get away from me before it's too late." My friend stared at me with certainty.

It was hard to walk away from Pablo, the last thing I wanted to do. But I left him, with the smell of violence in the air.

I walked as far as I could, trying to contain myself until I got to the opposite side of the yard. I didn't want to see what would happen.

Almost an hour passed. Then all the nerves in my body quivered at the sound of a prison alarm shrieking like an out-of-control bullhorn on the lower yard. I heard rapid gunshots. Pow! Pow! . . . Pow! Pow! Pow! Pow! Pow! . . . Pow! Pow! The shots came from a gun tower not far from where I had talked with Pablo. A guardsman's rifle was pointing down at the spot where I had stood. I knew instantly that Pablo was dead. My mind froze.

It was days later, after the prison came off a major lockdown that kept all of us confined to our cells for investigation, when I found out what had happened. Pablo had been stabbed eighteen times, and shot once in the thigh by one of the tower gunmen. He was pronounced dead in the prison hospital.

A friend who had witnessed the stabbing told me, "He was

crazy. He never stopped fighting. They told him to stop, but he kept going. It was like he was chasing death, and wasn't going to stop, no way, until he caught it—until he rode it on out of here."

A week later, I lay on my bunk, trying to find words for Alice. I wanted to write a beautiful letter saying what I thought her father had wanted to express.

Until that night, I had never opened the envelope I had taken from Pablo's pocket, because I didn't want to come face to face with her. What right did I have when I should be dead with him?

I finally brought it out of hiding and looked at the photograph. I could see in the dim light of my cell that Alice was a lovely girl with a strong resemblance to her father. I stared at the picture for some time, trying to compose a letter in my mind. Then I turned it over. The writing was barely legible:

Dear Alice,

Your Dad loves you. When you get this, my troubled life will have probably ended. But certainly not my love. Alice, with this photo, please know how I've always held on to you, and have kept you always in my heart. I love you. So take care, my darling, and please forgive me for all my wrongs. I wasn't a real father to you.

Love, Pablo

Pablo had already said it all.

THE MAN WHO TALKS TO HIMSELF

"Say, Mookie," I said from the next cell. "Now I see who you be talking to these days. When I walked past your cell, I seen you standing at the back, looking at all those pictures, goin' on and on."

"Yeah," said Mookie, laughing. "They're who I be kickin' it with. Can you hear me over there?"

"Man!" I said. "I hear you day in and day out—holding long conversations—and I'm beginning to think you're losing your damn mind."

"Nah, man," Mookie said. "It's not like that. You see, all these beautiful women I got here on my wall, they're a part of me—this is my posse, man!"

"You losing it, Mookie," I said. "I really think you're falling off the deep end."

"Nah, man," Mookie said. "I know all these women personally."

"Those pictures been torn out of magazines," I said. "So don't drag on me that you know any of these women personally. That's a bunch of bullshit."

"That's not what I'm saying," Mookie said.

"Well, what are you saying?"

"Well, it's a thing like this," Mookie said. "Now you take for example the picture you caught me kickin' it with when you walked by my cell. Her name is Marie. When I seen her in *Vogue* magazine, I clipped her out of the lime-life and brought her into my world. I asked her did she want to be a part of me, and she said yeah—so I placed her on my wall."

"So what you're telling me," I said, "is that all these women you got on your wall agreed to be a part of you?"

"Yeah . . . yeah," Mookie said. "Man, now you're getting it. But check: none of them know each other. They're all different, with different personalities."

"How do you know that none of them know each other?" I asked Mookie.

"Man, because they all come out of different magazines. It'd be stupid for me to be involved with two, three, or five women and they all know each other."

"Well, OK," I said, "but what do you mean by saying they're all different?"

"Let's take Marie for an example," Mookie explained. "She's my old lady, man. All she wants me to do is stay at home, and she's always buggin' me about fixing shit around the house. She's a good woman, don't get me wrong. Whenever I need to talk about my future, our future, she's the one I spend time kickin' it with. We been trying to have a baby for the past year."

"Is that right?" I said.

"Yeah, man, and you know something else? Marie is the only woman I can trust with my money. She pays all the bills and shit like that. That woman has a real good heart, you know?"

"You're really serious, aren't you?" I asked.

"Why would I lie?" Mookie replied. "It's the truth—Marie is a good woman."

"No, I wasn't talking about that—well, never mind," I said. "Mook, you know something, you're crazy."

"I'm not crazy," he said. "I'm just serving you with the Real. I just got it goin' on over here."

"OK, OK," I said. "Now what about all those other pictures on your wall—what about them?"

Mookie laughed. "I met Suzie at a bar. She loves to party,

likes fast cars, and is always trying to get me to spend money on her slick self. She's basically materialistic. And man, she's a total freak! The only good thing about Suzie is having her on my arm when I go to parties. I love her, but she's not my everyday type."

"What do you mean, she isn't your everyday type?" I asked.

"Well, she's cool and all that," Mookie said, "but she's just a little bit too fast and wild. Plus, she's forever wanting things—perfume and fur coats and all that stuff."

"So where did you get her picture?"

"Oh, I got her out of *Hustler* magazine."

"Who were you talking to last night?" I asked Mookie. "I heard you talking to somebody."

"Ummm . . . who was I talking to?" Mookie mumbled. "Oh, I know, I was kickin' it with Debbie."

"Who's Debbie?"

"Debbie is in college. I been with her for about nine months."

"Well, what was you guys talking about last night?"

"I was trying to convince her to stay in school. She wanted to quit. The thing about Debbie is that she has a real good head on her shoulders, and all she really needs is encouragement."

"How did you meet her?"

"I was Debbie's first love," Mookie said. "She's the one I think of the most."

"Why is that?"

"She lets me in on her decisions, and she listens to all my opinions. She listens to me a lot more than to anyone else, I suppose."

"So where did you get her picture?" I asked.

"I got her out of *Playboy*."

"Tell me something, Mookie," I said. "Do you know all these other women as well as you know the ones you've told me about?"

"Oh, yeah," said Mookie. "I know every single one. Man, looka here, I wouldn't have a woman's picture on my wall if I didn't know her. That would be crazy."

"It would?" I asked.

"Yeah, crazy. Man, I'm not crazy. Sometimes when you hear me talking, I may sound a little crazy, especially when I'm arguing with Loretta."

"Who's Loretta?" I asked.

"Oh, man," said Mookie. "Loretta is a hardheaded female that got my baby."

"Where did you get her picture from?"

"Man, I got her out of *Penthouse* magazine. But, anyway, that don't make me crazy. I been talking to 'em, my women, for the past five years, after being here for ten. People think I'm crazy, but now you know I'm not."

"Well, how do I 'posed to know this?" I asked Mookie.

"Because now you know who I be talking to," Mookie said. "You see, only the fools who can hear me but don't know who I'm talking to are the ones that thinks I'm crazy. And I'm not. Jarvis, man, if I was, I wouldn't have anyone to talk to. Hey, I would just be talking to myself. You see, that's crazy," he said. "Tha . . . that's crazy!"

A REASON TO LIVE

"Man, I wonder why that dude Alex keeps trying to kill himself," Tex said to me as we stood along the fence one hot summer day out on the exercise yard. "In Texas, where I come from, boy, black folks thank the Lawd, I mean daily, that white folks ain't lynching there no more. And here we are, man, in the eighties, standing right in the middle of San Quentin, staring at this young black man that's out trying to lynch himself. I tell ya, that boy needs his damn ass whipped!"

"Is that him over there," I asked, "with the basketball?"

"Yep, that's him," said Tex. "That boy is one sad case if I ever seen one. All he need, man, is one of those royal ass whippings, that's all!"

"Naw," I replied, "I don't think that's going to solve anything. He just needs to sit down with one of us who's been here a few years and get schooled on how to cope with all this prison madness."

"Man, don't you know I spent four long aching hours talking to this dude the last time he tried committing suicide? We sat right there in that corner, man, rapping about what was going on. Shuh! It didn't do no good, though, because in two weeks, not even two weeks, that nut went and tried it again. That pisses me off."

"Well, hey, you probably didn't get at him right. You probably did all this gabbing, thinking he was listening when he wasn't. You know how young dudes are. They only hear what they want to."

"Nah, man," said Tex, "it wasn't nothin' like that. I really approached him with good intentions. I went all out trying to give this young brother the benefit of my experience."

"Is that right?" I asked.

"Ah, man! When I found out for the first time that a youngster in this building had tried to take himself out by the back door, it really hurt me. I rose straight out of my bunk, smoked half a pack of cigarettes, and decided right then that I was going to try to convince him that suicide wasn't cool."

"When you first got wind of it, did you know who he was?" I asked.

"The only thing I got off the grapevine that night was that a young con had tried to hang himself in our cell block but was cutted down in time by the guards. It wasn't until the following morning that I found out it was Alex."

"So how long after this did you have an opportunity to get with him?"

"He spent a few days in the prison psych ward before they brought his tail back to the cell block. I think it was about a week after his first attempt that we sat down in the yard."

"Did he ever tell you why he tried to take himself out?" I asked.

"Oh, yeah," Tex said. "We kicked that at length. This dude is only eighteen years old. But trip out: he told me it was because his girlfriend stood him up two weeks in a row."

"What?" I shouted. "Is that all? Tex, you must be jiving. You really don't mean to tell me this fool tried to kill himself just because his girlfriend stood him up? Is he nuts or just straight-out stupid?"

"Man, I don't have the slightest idea. All I know is what he said. And he told me that she stopped writing him, too."

"How much time did this fool say he had left?"

"Jarvis, man, you ain't going to believe it. This guy only have, get this, eleven more months left. Man, he is only doing wino time."

"It must be his cell that is really getting to him, huh?"

"Hell, no. That boy got boo-coo people to write and mo' appliances than I ever had and I been in S.Q. almost eight years," Tex said with envy. "That dude has a lot mo' people than me who really cares for him on the outside. They already sent him a color TV and a radio."

"So what's his problem?"

"Hey, man, your guess is better than mine. All I know is, I sat there talking to this dude for hours, sharing all my experiences and trying to give him, you know, the strength to live."

"Did he listen?"

"Oh, yeah, he listened, but what got rocks in my jaws is that afterwards he turns around—and I mean right around—and tries to hang himself again."

"Maybe, Tex, he just wants attention."

"Well, if that's what he's after," said Tex, "he damn sho' ain't going to find it in San Quentin. Hell! This here don't look nothin' like no Betty Ford's center."

"Tell me this," I said, "did he come real close to dying both times or did it seem he wasn't for real?"

"Man, he was most definitely serious," Tex said. "From word off the grapevine, the boy really wants to die, man!"

"Is that right?" I said, lighting a cigarette. We stood in silence, staring at Alex across the exercise yard. In any other place, he would have looked like a typical high school teenager.

"Hey, Tex," I said, after a while. "Check it out: I'm going to call this Alex dude over here and try to reach his senses on this, because, man, if I don't and he ends up killing himself, I'm going to feel terrible that I never tried."

"Jay, it ain't going to do no good. Man, you know just as well as I do this dude is going to do whatever he wants, so why try?"

"You may be right, but at least I'll be able to say, like you, that I tried."

"But why repeat everything I already said? Anything you tell him is going to go in one ear and out the other."

"No, Tex, I don't think so. I'm going to approach it differently. And we really don't have nothing to lose."

"What do you mean?"

"You'll see. Just hang out with me while I talk to him, OK?"

"Yeah, but I bet you anything," said Tex, "he's going to smile and nod, acting like he did when I was trying to pour some sense into his empty head. But man, this boy is high on a serious death wish."

"Well, let's just find out."

I called Alex over.

"How you be?" I asked.

"I'm doing pretty good." He stared at me curiously, leaning his shoulder on the fence.

"Hey, check. My name is Jarvis. Tex here has told me that you are the youngster making all the headlines around this joint—trying to do a hari-kari on us—so I thought I better hurry up and introduce myself before you fool around again and get it right, you dig?"

"Uh-huh," Alex nodded. "I hear where you're comin' from."

"Now, Bro," I said, "I don't mean to half-step you with a lot of shuffle 'n 'jive—this is the real deal, the real McCoy, you dig?"

"Yeah, yeah. I hear you," Alex muttered, looking bored.

"I'm told that you only been in the prison system a short while. Is that right?"

"No, that ain't right." Alex pulled away from the fence. "I been in for 'bout six months."

"Yeah, OK!" I grinned. "That is just what I mean. For me, six months is short—in fact, so short that if you were a wino, you'd still have alcohol on your breath. Bro, let me tell you somethin'. Unlike Tex here, I personally don't care what you do. And you can wipe the bored expression off your face, dude. You can kill your damn self tonight and I'll snore right through it, you dig? I don't give a mad fuck! And most cons in this joint have the same attitude. We wouldn't give a rat's ass about what you do, you dig?

"Now, aside from that, I think you were really fortunate that Tex spent his entire yard time a few weeks back trying to give you all the benefits of his experience. Because he knows why it is important for you to stay alive."

"Hey, Bro," said Alex, trying to explain. "I understood what Tex was saying that day—I'm just having problems with my wom—"

"Whoa! I need to cut you off right there." I shook my head angrily. "We don't need to get into all the whys, man. Trip: I'm not here, like Tex, to persuade you not to kill your damn self—no way! In fact, I was just tellin' him I kind of wished your cell was next to mine whenever you try that foolishness again."

"Huh?" Alex was puzzled.

"He is serious!" said Tex. "Dead serious!"

"You goddamn right!" I said. "Why wouldn't I be? The way I see it, I would get all your food—your breakfast, your lunch, and that hot dinner—because, hell, everybody knows it doesn't make a lot of sense to eat on the eve of killing yourself. At the morgue, before they embalm your young stupid ass they just going to cut your stomach open and take it all out and dump it, anyway. So if I was in the next cell, you wouldn't have no qualms about sliding me over all your grub, huh?"

"Man," Alex took a second and swallowed. "I don't know too much about all that."

"That's what they do to all the stiffs. But moving along, don't you have a brand new color TV and radio in your cell?"

"Uh-huh . . . that my folks got for me."

"Well, hey, Alex, I don't mean to sound rude, but instead of giving the prison first grabs at 'em—you know they're theirs after you kill yourself—why not let me have 'em? That would be cool."

"No way, man. I am keeping my TV and radio."

"How's that? You thinking about having someone put 'em in your coffin?" I retorted.

"No," said Alex. "I'm keeping my things, though."

"You don't understand, Alex," I said. "I don't want 'em right now. No, man, I'm talking 'bout before you clamp that rope around your neck the next time—right before you kick the box under your feet and get to dangling 'round on your air vent, jerkin' and kickin' your feet against the back wall of your cell, all that saliva dribbling out your mouth and those big, fat snot bubbles blowing from your nose.

"Man!" I began laughing. "I bet that'd be real fun to watch—just seeing your feet vibrating, you turning purple in the face, then watching you hang deader than a doorknob on your vent . . . Man, man, man! What I want, though, is that color TV you got. So, Bro, how 'bout it?"

"Man, you are crazy," Alex stuttered, his eyes open wide, as he backpedaled away. "Uh-uh, I'm keeping my TV. You crazy, dude!"

"Aw, man!" I said. "What is it wit' you? Why are you calling me crazy? I never said that suicide was crazy. I mean, whatever is right for you is all right with me, too. I just want first cracks at your TV. What's wrong wit' that?"

"No, man. No way!" Alex stared, terrified. "You dudes is crazy. Man, you can't have my TV." He shook, looking for an out.

"Wait a minute," I said. "Where are you going? I haven't finished talkin' to you, Bro!"

"Man, I'm gettin' on," said Alex. "You's nuts. I swear you dudes is crazy."

"Before you go 'bout your business," I said, "check it: how 'bout them tennies you have on? You should at least let me have them."

"No way!" Alex stared down at his shoes. "I just got these Nikes last week. You can't have these for all the world."

"Those aren't Nikes. Let me see," I said, stepping toward him. "Wow, they are Nikes!" I snatched Alex by his coat and quickly pinned him to the fence. "Listen, you young chump." My eyes stared inches from the frightened kid's face. "You don't know nothin' 'bout this world. Trying to kill yourself—you don't know shit—and you know what? Since I still got big plans for being on this here planet, dude, you going to give me those damn shoes.

"Say, Tex," I said, turning. "Take off this chump's shoes. He's a dead man anyway, so fuck him and feed him fish. Man, get his damn shoes off."

"Man . . . are you serious?" asked Tex, stunned.

"Hell, yeah!" I shouted. "This chump don't need no shoes where he wants to go." Tex crouched down to remove Alex's shoes.

"No, please don't," Alex begged. "Please don't take my shoes."

"Chump, shut up!" I threatened, wondering if Alex would find the will to fight.

"Man, let me go!" Alex burst out, shoving and gritting his teeth like a threatened wild animal until I gave way, letting him break loose. "Man, you dudes is fuckin' crazy!" he yelled, storming across the yard, his shoes unlaced.

"Ah, man, come on back here. I still have some mo' rap—"

"Hell, naw!" he screamed, staring over his shoulder.

"Well," I said, "just hurry up and take care of that business, so I can watch me some color TV. It's mine when you kill yourself. So don't take too long."

"You know what? Fuck you!" Alex shouted bravely from the middle of the exercise yard. "Your ass will die before mine's—and guess who is going to get your TV? I am! So you hurry up wit' your own damn business, you crazy nut."

"Oh, yeah? We just have to see about that."

I turned to Tex. "What do you think?"

"You wanna know what I think?" said Tex, flabbergasted. "I think you're crazier than all outdoors—tellin' that young'un about danglin' on his vent and saliva dribblin' out his mouth and that snot bubble in his nose. Ugh! Damn, where 'bout did you get all that crazy stuff?"

"Man, I don't know. I needed to reach that dude."

"Were you serious, though? Is that what happens when someone hangs themself?"

"I don't know. I never seen anyone hang himself. All I wanted to do is give this boy a reason to live. So do you think he'll try it again?"

"Hell no, he ain't goin' to try no shit like that again. Didn't you see his eyes? Man, he was scared shitless."

"Is that right?" I chuckled.

"I'm tellin' you, the boy was so scared of killing himself that I wouldn't doubt it if he outlives us both. This boy wants to live—if for nothin' else, to see your butt die before his."

"You know something, Tex?" I said as we looked out across the exercise yard. "That was the best damn 'Fuck you' I ever heard."

FRUITCAKES

When the cell doors slammed shut behind me and I found myself on the south side of the first tier in the security housing unit, I didn't know what to expect. I only understood that I had been relocated to what was considered the "crazy tier" by some, and the worst place in San Quentin by everyone. I was in the worst of the worst.

The cell stank—mostly from a fat dead rat floating in the toilet. It took several flushes to send it spinning down.

"Hey, man," a voice whispered from the adjacent cell. "What's your name? Can you spare a smoke?"

"No," I said, "I don't have none. My name's Jarvis. What's yours?"

"Joe," the voice said. "I'm in cell sixty, right next to you. You sure you can't spare a smoke?"

"Yeah, I'm sure," I said. "I wish I had some right about now! I guess they let you guys smoke down here, huh?"

"Well," he hesitated. "Not really. But sometimes, every blue moon or so, someone will keister a good issue of tobacco before they come down here. Man! I need a fuckin' cigarette! How about a butt, huh?"

"I wish I could help you, Joe, but I really don't have none," I said. It was hard to believe inmates actually keistered tobacco here. In all my years in San Quentin, I'd never heard of anyone smuggling tobacco in their rectum!

"Hey, Joe," hollered another voice from down the tier. "Save me shorts on that cigarette."

"Who's that?" asked Joe.

"Man!" he said. "This is ol' Cal and his dog, Spot! Send us shorts on that cigarette."

"Say, Dude!" Joe yelled down the tier. "You heard my neighbor just say he didn't have any. So get up off me, motherfucker!"

"Now, Joe!" said Cal. "My dog don't care for all that profanity. Go get 'em, boy . . . sic 'em! . . . kill, dog, kill!" Cal barked at the top of his lungs and it sounded real.

"Punk," Joe shouted. "I'll kill you and that damn dog!"

"Shut up!" another voice interrupted. "Lay your fruitcake asses down."

"Ah, Angry Bear," said Joe. "You best shut up, too. You ain't kickin' up no dust! Man, I'm the hog wit' the big nut sack around here."

"Man, all you doin' is frontin'," said Bear, "trying to act like you somethin', all because you got a new neighbor and cravin' yo' punk ass off for a smoke. That's all."

"Man!" Joe yelled. "Let me tell yo' punk ass somethin' . . ."

The yelling went back and forth, and it seemed the whole tier had gone berserk. So while I was cleaning out my cell, I learned about the people around me. I heard everybody's name at least once, I learned what they accused each other of being in prison for, which psych medications they were on, and which of them were racists.

But for all of this they liked the tier just fine. There were no rules—there wasn't even a difference between night and day. They could be as crazy as they wanted, say anything they wanted, do anything they wanted, and disrespect whomever they pleased—including the prison guards, who saw the uselessness of writing disciplinary charges for any of the prison rule violations. In a way, this was the prisoners' own tier, and nobody had anything to say about it.

"Where did all these crazy people come from?" I wondered. At first it seemed as though everyone was hollering, but as I listened I realized that only six or seven of the seventeen inmates on the tier were yelling.

The small square windows high on the upper walls were open about a foot. This was their full extent. They were there more for ventilation than for light or scenery. Only by standing on the concrete slab that was my bed could I see whether it was day or night. The metal mesh that covered the windows made looking out unpleasant; it seemed as though bars had been placed on the sky. The view was no more than a clock to guess the time of day.

I didn't know how long it had taken me to get settled in my new living situation or how long the yelling had been going on before I turned to the front of my cell and saw an old man roaming around on the tier. He acted as if he were lost. His light blue suit and red hat and rubber sneakers puzzled me. For sure, he was not a guard. All the correctional officers wore green jumpsuits. "Who in God's name is he?" I wondered. "And how on earth can he be so lost, standing in the middle of the most secure cell block in San Quentin?"

Surrounded by what sounded like the roar of a football stadium, the old man inched up to my cell bars.

"Hi, cell fifty-nine," he seemed glad to say. "Please forgive me, but I forgot my specs this morning, and I'm having problems locating cell numbers. How are you today?" he asked and then went on talking. "I have some new stuff for you. I got your note about the side effects, so I want you to try these."

"Hold on a minute!" I interrupted. "Man, are you sure you're talking about me? Who are you, anyway? I don't think you have the right cell."

"I'm one of the prison psychiatrists," he said. "This is cell fifty-nine, isn't it?" Then taking a step back and squinting at the number above, he smiled.

"Yeah, yeah!" he said. "I got your note about Thorazine and the side effects. Not too many people like them, but here, I want you to try these."

The psychiatrist reached into his inside coat pocket and pulled out several multicolored syringes. I was speechless. I never thought I'd see a psychiatrist carrying syringes in the pocket of his coat.

"Gee, these will definitely make you feel real good up the road," he said, "but they aren't for you now. What I do have for you," he mumbled, "let's see . . . they must be in one of my other pockets . . ."

This time the psychiatrist reached into his pants pocket. I couldn't believe my eyes. Was this how the state distributed legal drugs?

"Ahhh! Here we go!" he said finally, staring down at a handful of pills. "Wow—all these delicious treats! Of course, you can't have 'em all—we don't want that, do we?—but this baby here, I'm sure, is the one for you."

"Hold on! Hold on, Doc!" I said. "I'm not on any medication . . . I don't think. I know you don't have the right cell here. Man, are you sure you have the right person?"

"Well . . . well," the psych hesitated. "Just how long have you been in this cell?" he asked.

"Hours, Doc! Only a few hours!"

"What's your last name and number?"

"Masters, C-35169," I answered quickly.

"Oh! Well, then!" he said, checking a list retrieved from yet another pocket. I began wondering about this psych's pockets.

Everything he had pulled out of them so far had scared the dickens out of me.

"Hmmm, my man must have transferred," he resolved, scratching his butt. "How are you, though? The noise here must be disturbing. If you like I can give you something while I'm here, so you can get through the night."

"No, no!" I said. "I'm doing fine, sir!"

"Well, let's see . . . ," he said, reaching into one of his pants pockets. "How about this tiny blue one. This is Mellaril. But I also have . . . let's see, Prolixin and Cogentin. But these here," he admitted with a doctor's frown, "I'm not so sure of. Most folks prefer these blue Mellaril to the Sinequan," he said, almost as if talking to himself. "I totally agree! So . . . let's start you off here, and you can let me know how you feel. I'm usually down here twice a week. Do you have a cup?" he asked. "Because I have to see you take the medication."

"No, Doc!" I said. "I mean, which part of 'no' do you not understand, huh? That stuff you have is for crazy people and I don't want any."

"Nonsense!" he said. "Of course you do. Here, take two."

"No! No!" I insisted. "Why don't you take your pockets filled with syringes and funny pills some damn place else?"

"Well, sir," he said, "you don't have to get smart!"

"Of course I do, because you, sir, are not listening."

"Well, then," he said, "I'm sorry I couldn't be of any help to you today. But I'll be back on the tier later in the week—so if you happen to need any help sleeping or whatever, just let me know. By the way, fellow, do you have a television?"

"Why?" I shouted in his face.

"Used to be a time," he explained, "before the inmates had televisions in their cells, when they all requested to see me.

Today, it's different. And that's too bad. So, so bad." And he walked away down the tier.

Not long after I'd been relocated, the evening chow cart came rolling down the tier. The guards started with the end cell and moved toward the front. They unlocked each cell's food port and gave the prisoner whatever portion of food he wanted from the cart. Today was Mexican food, my favorite.

When the cart was just a few cells away from mine, I saw a hand lunge out of an open port and fling a cup of urine and feces into the faces of the two guards serving the food. It took a few seconds before I could believe my eyes and nose. The guards stood there with faces dripping, their serving spatulas still in their hands. Then a maniacal laugh broke the silence.

"Eat my shit! I saved that from yesterday when you punks didn't give me no shitwipe. Now both of you can just eat it!"

"You'll pay for this," one of the guards said calmly, and the two of them hurried off the tier with the food cart.

"You did it now!" said Joe. "They'll be back to beat the Rodney-King-shit out of you, Walter!"

"Who cares? I need an ass kicking anyways." He started laughing. "Did you guys see that? Those two punks was smacking on my shit. I did that for you guys, too," he added.

"You did that on your own," Joe yelled. "We didn't ask for no toilet paper yesterday. So don't try to pull us into it. It's bad enough you fucked off all the damn food!"

"Hey, Joe, you mean we don't get to eat tonight?" I asked.

"Yeah, you'll eat," he said, "if you want to eat off a cart with Walter's shit all over it."

"You ain't serious, are you?"

"Listen, man, we're just a bunch of fruitcakes down here. We don't have nothin' comin' tonight! That's the bottom line—not unless you want to eat Walter's shit!"

"Ah, man," said Walter. "None of what I threw hitted the food cart. It hitted the cops."

"Man," shouted Joe, "you's a damn lie! That fuckin' shit hitted everything—I hope they kick yo' teeth in, punk."

About an hour later I heard what sounded like an army of guards preparing to enter the tier: there were lots of keys jingling and the guards' shields clanking and the huge plastic emergency gurney rattling as it was taken off the wall.

Then a dozen guards marched past my cell dressed in full armored gear, with helmets and batons, and riot shields held tightly to their chests. The unit sergeant had a Taser, a stun gun, and several other guards carried block guns, which shoot a high-velocity wooden block that can severely disable a person.

They gathered in front of Walter's cell. When I stood close to my cell bars, I could just see down the tier to where they were. The unit sergeant had opened the food port, then shouted the order for Walter to step to his cell door immediately to be handcuffed.

"Are you going to cuff up?" he demanded.

Walter's response was quick. "Yes, sir! I don't want any problems. I am fully cooperating. I'm not resisting."

"That's not fast enough," said the sergeant. He stepped aside to give the gunmen a clear shot into the port of Walter's cell. The gun blasts sounded like shotguns. Pow! Pow! Then the electric cell door came open, and the guards rushed inside. The whole tier heard the beating and Walter's screams. I could smell his flesh burning from the Taser device.

They went on beating Walter until the screams stopped and their kicks and punches sounded like thuds on a corpse.

"Throw his ass on the gurney," the sergeant ordered. The guards dragged Walter out of his cell. They used only their booted feet to get him onto the gurney, just a few feet from my cell. There was blood everywhere. The guards' adrenaline rush seemed to have passed. They were probably thinking about HIV and not wanting to be contaminated by Walter's blood, though many of them already had blood on their clothing.

They finally got Walter on the gurney, then lifted it up. As they started down the tier, a guard called, "Wait a minute," and picked something up from the floor. "Here's some of the bastard's teeth," he said, and threw them onto the gurney. I will never forget the sound they made, like craps being thrown against a wooden ledge.

There were no witnesses to this other than us "fruitcakes." As far as I could tell, none of the others gave any thought to it. Later, guards mopped up the blood and everyone went back to the routine of hollering back and forth. There was no mention of dinner.

One evening, as darkness fell and I was wishing for nothing else to happen, it did.

I smelled toxic fumes on the tier. Thin wisps of gray smoke were leaking out of the "quiet cells." These are the last six cells on the tier, used for solitary confinement. They are called "quiet" because each cell is reinforced with a steel-plated door and there are no windows. The idea is not to make it quiet for the inmate, but to keep the inmate's sounds, like screaming, from being heard. Water is rationed; every eight hours the toilet and sink are turned on for a short time, then turned back off.

Standing at my cell bars, I could see flames coming from one of the quiet cells. The smoke began to thicken.

I wasn't sure of the prisoners' rules here. I didn't know to mind my own business or pretend, as everyone else seemed to be doing, that nothing was going on. When I heard someone yelling for help, I wanted to holler over the noise on the tier to the guards, to tell them there was a fire in one of the quiet cells. I was certain that everybody smelled what I did and I couldn't imagine why nobody was saying anything. These were fruitcakes, I thought. That was why.

Now came the awful smell of burning paint. The thick layers of paint on the walls of this old prison were catching fire. I hid my coughs in a pillow.

"Hey, Joe," I said, choking. "Can't you smell that fire in the back?"

"Yeah, that's that dumb ass Jack Marbol in cell sixty-three. He's trying to get out of his cell. He just wants to take a night stroll to the hospital . . . to see the pretty nurses."

"He's going to die back there," I said. "Don't you think we better call the cops?"

"No," said Joe. "If you do, he'll do the same thing next week, and we'll all be chokin' again. The last time he set his cell on fire, we all helped to get the guards down here, but we told him if he ever did this shit again, we'd just let his punk ass die!"

"How many times has he done this?" I asked.

"He does this shit every week, man. He's going to kill us all someday. But he's going to learn this time."

"Yeah, by dying, if we don't help him."

"Nah, he'll be OK," said Joe. "Don't worry. Sooner or later the goons will get a whiff of this and they'll come and drag his fat ass out."

No sooner had Joe said this than the guards entered the tier. They were the same two guards who had been hit with human waste, so I wasn't surprised that they weren't in any great rush. They walked down the tier, taking their routine body count.

When they got to the fire, they appeared to ignore it, and then strolled away, as if to say, "Let him die."

But minutes later they returned equipped with gas masks and carrying small fire extinguishers. "There's more smoke than fire," one of them said, spraying the smoke-filled cell.

I couldn't see anything. I could only hear one of the guards shouting, "Hey, Jack Marbol. Come on, guy . . . you want out of this cell, you're going to have to let us handcuff you. Step over here to the front of your cell. Step up . . . step up to the bars . . . listen! We can't get you out of there until you let us cuff you up."

The attitude of some of the guards is to wear leather gloves for the so-called bad-ass prisoners and silk ones for those who will "cooperate." It seemed like Jack Marbol got silk gloves that day.

"There you go," said the other guard. "Move closer . . . there you go. Are you burned anywhere? We'll have you out of there in no time now.

"Clear on cell sixty-three!" he hollered to a guard who controlled the electric bar gate.

"Stand clear!" the gate guard yelled back. He opened the cell door. A minute passed.

"Close cell sixty-three," yelled the guards.

"Stand clear!" came the answer. "Sixty-three now coming closed!"

"There you go," one of the guards said to Jack Marbol, and I saw that they held him up by the arms.

"Whoa! Whoa! Take it easy . . . take it easy . . . let me lead you . . . watch your step."

I watched Jack Marbol, dressed only in undershorts, as he struggled to walk. Then he collapsed on the tier, in front of my cell. He fell to his knees, retching. His white body and face were charred black, like those of a coal miner trapped in a mine shaft.

The whole tier began laughing up a storm, and some said they wished Jack Marbol would die right there on the spot.

I stared into his eyes, and saw a person's heart on fire. No matter how the others laughed or what they wished for, I vowed that as one nut in this very large fruitcake I would never be cracked. I prayed that ol' Jack Marbol, a prisoner like myself, would be OK.

THIRTEEN SIXTY-EIGHT

"That damn psych really likes to get on my nerves," said Milton, talking to himself in the next cell. He called over to me, "Hey, Jarvis, did you hear what he was asking me?"

"No, not really," I answered, lying on my bunk. "I only heard bits and pieces of it. I'm too heavy into this book."

"Man! Don't you know," Milton complained, "that old geezer had the nerve to sneak up on me and just stand in front of my cell, not saying a word, just lookin' at me with those weird eyes of his, like I'm crazy."

"Who's that?" I asked, trying to follow the story line of my book.

"Man, that psych!" shouted Milton. "I forget his name, but you done seen him before. He's the one always walkin' around this prison dress' in a dingy ol' suit two sizes smaller than him, with a stained pipe that's never lit stuck in his mouth. He never lights that damn pipe."

"Yeah, I know the one." I smiled. "So what does he be asking you?"

"Man, he keeps asking me some really crazy shit. Every week for the past month he comes to my bars, stands out there on the tier, and says, 'How are you doing? Are they treating you all right? Do you need anything to help you sleep?'—things like that. I mean, what the hell is his problem?"

"Well, I don't know, maybe he's just checking up on you."

"Nah, it ain't that. He's trying to get inside my head," Milton shouted. "The motherfucker is trying to toy with my goddamn brain. He already thinks I'm thirteen sixty-eight."

"What's that?" I asked.

"That's some legal phrase they use in all the courtrooms I been in to mean crazy."

"Well?" I asked. "What do you think, are you crazy?"

"No," Milton hesitated. "Not for San Quentin. Man, to have lived in this prison as long as I have, eleven years, and most of it in isolation, I can't be no more insane than this prison—or that psych. He's been here a lot longer than I have. Look at him."

"The psych goes home each day," I said. "But what about you, could you make it out there in society, Milton?"

"Hell, nah!" Milton sounded insulted. "Man, don't you know that in these past eleven years I have lived like a mad wounded elephant? I have been shot, shot at, hit with clubs, blackjacked, gassed, choked, Tasered, cut, bruised, and stabbed four times!"

"Damn, is that right?" I set my book aside. "Is that right?"

"Man, right nothin'! Listen, that ain't half of it. I have been jumped on, tromped on, spit on, had some of my teeth kicked out, and a few ribs broken. I've had piss and shit thrown in my face. I've been match-bombed, fire-bombed, electrocuted, and blow-darted more times than I care to remember—even been poisoned once. Then beaten, thrown, dragged, and slammed in and out of these isolation holes so many times that it felt like I seen the whole fuckin' world come to an end."

"Well, what happen' when you seen the world end?" I asked.

"Man, shit! That's when I knew this had to be hell, and you know something?" Milton laughed in rage. "I was right. This is hell. This is hell if you never seen it before."

"So why don't you want to leave?" I asked. "It doesn't make much sense staying in hell, does it?"

"Oh, I want to leave all right," said Milton. "Man, I can't wait to leave. Yes, sir, all they have to do is spring me loose, and boy oh boy, when they do, I made only one promise to myself—not to do anything that nobody hasn't done to me. Man, you know what I'm sayin'? Hey, check: fair exchange can't be called a robbery. Yep! It sure can't." Milton slammed his fist into his hand.

"I was askin' that psych a while ago," he went on, "why everybody is so afraid of me getting released."

"And what did he say?"

"They're afraid because I'm going to be discharged so soon—next month."

"Man," I said, "you mean to tell me that you get out next month?"

"Oh, yes!" Milton chuckled, slamming his fist harder into his hand. "Oh, yeah. Oh, yeah." He went on repeating "Oh, yeah!" to the rhythm of his slamming fist.

THE BONEYARD VISIT

Herbert's cell had been empty for three days when he finally returned home to the second tier. "Man, how did it go?" I asked, hearing his cell door slam shut behind him.

"Hey, Bro," said Herbert. "It was cool. Man, it couldn't have been better. Some crazy shit happen' though, on that first night. But I'll tell you about it later—just give me a few ticks so I can put my stuff up and tighten up my cell a bit."

"Give me a holler when you get finish'," I said, elated thinking about what my neighbor's first conjugal visit must have been like. His wife, Joyce, with whom he had been corresponding for eight years and whom he had married in prison just a year ago, was the first woman Herbert had been with for more than thirteen years.

"Hey, Jay," Herbert later called over to me. "What can I say, except that these boneyard visits is really cool."

"So you like it, huh?" I smiled. "Tell me about it. Was you nervous? Man, I just know you had to be nervous."

"Shit, yeah, I was nervous," said Herb. "Man, I was so damn 'noid walking over to those trailers that I was hopin' somebody would say my visit was canceled."

"Is that right, Herb?" I laughed as my excitement moved me to the front of my cell. "So what happen' when you got there?"

"Joyce was already there, and when I walks inside she says, 'Hi, Sugar, are you glad to see me, Daddy?'"

"And what did you say?"

"Ah, man, I just smiled and told her that I was. Then we

hugged each other and the guard who escorted me left us by ourselves."

"Is that right? Then what happen', Herb?"

"Well, Joyce had this pamphlet in her hand. She said the guards wanted us to read it. It was just rules, all the dos and don'ts."

"What did the rules say?"

"Shit, man, I forget. I ain't never been good at remembering rules. I just tells Joyce, 'Say, Baby, let's sit down and read these rules so we'll know what's happening'—you know, as a way of trying to get this woman to chill out. Because in no time, she was just a'nibblin' all over a guy's neck and wantin' to make love. She wasn't wasting no time, man. No time!"

"Is that right?" I said, still smiling. "So you wasn't ready for anything, huh?"

"Man, let me tell you something." Herbert got animated and came closer to the front of his cell. "Don't you know I wasn't ready for nothing! Shit! Just being alone with that woman and no guards around was scary enough."

"Ah, man!" I joked. "I thought you was going to make some serious love for three days and nights—isn't that what you was tellin' me before you left? I just knew your ol' ass was going to freeze up. So what happen' next?"

"Well," said Herbert, "after about a hour or so of reading those damn rules—"

"What? You mean to tell me you spent a whole hour reading those goddamn rules, Herb? Man, what's wrong with you? You haven't read no rules since you been in San Quentin—and here you go on your honeymoon, of all places, reading rules. Man, are you crazy?"

Herbert laughed. "Jay, you just don't know how it was being in that big-ass trailer—it had to be five times the size of our cells.

Shit, what would you do alone in a place that big after thirteen years? I really did think I was goin' to go off and make passionate love to Joyce like I was tellin' y'all—but man, on that first day, it was totally strange. Even as Joyce got to sweet talkin' me and wantin' to live it up, I was afraid of bein' with that woman after all these years of just beatin' off and shit—what can I say? I guess the honest-to-God truth is my swipe wouldn't even get hard. Can you believe that? I damn sure wasn't goin' to take off my clothes and let Joyce get a bird's-eye view of my twitty bird."

"Is that right?" All the prisoners down the tier who'd been listening in started laughing at Herbert's truthful explanation.

"No way!" said Herbert. "And I had been braggin' to Joyce for years about what a big stud I am, about how I was going to rock her world, make some serious love to her if we ever got our chance. Don't you realize how damn embarrassing it would've been to take off my clothes, not having it up?"

"OK, Herb. I hear you." I tried not to crack up. "So what happen' next, homie?"

"Well, not too much of anything!" Herbert admitted. "By the time Baby and me puts away all the food that she brings for the three-day stay, we straight-kicks it for about an hour or two, just talkin' and cuddlin' up to each other. Now all the time, I'm starting to get pretty loose. So we ends up lockin' up, you know, kissin' and rollin' around on this huge-ass bed. Man, nothin' like these prison bunks."

"Yeah, I hear ya! So now you're ready, huh, big Herb?"

"Oh, yeah, I was." Herbert started to get boastful, standing at his cell door. "Man, my swipe got harder than this here penitentiary steel, like these cell bars, by the time I gets on top of Joyce. And man, just as I closed my eyes, getting a nice stroke and rhythm goin', in no time somethin' inside that woman grabbed my swipe and squeezed it like it had teeth, scarin' the holy living shit out of me. I screamed and jumped clean off this woman, tryin' to get my rabbit ass out of that damn bed. And them beds is wide, too. It seemed like I had to swim a mile to get off that bed. I went into straight panic, holdin' onto my swipe, tryin' to get my damn feet on the floor to get the hell out of there."

"Nah, you bullshitting, Herb?" Now the entire tier broke up. "Man, I know you can't be serious."

"I bullshit you not!" said Herbert. "This is the God's truth. Then trip: Joyce looks at me, lying way over there on the other side of the bed. In that sweet voice of hers she says, 'Daddy, what's wrong?'

"'What's wrong?' I said, standing at the bedroom door, butt naked. 'Girl, what in the world do you have up in you?'

"Joyce says, 'Is that what got you to jumpity-jump? Damn, Baby, I thought it was your heart or something.'

"I said, 'It's my heart now, but a second ago it was you! Girl, what was that?'

"She says, trying not to giggle, 'Those were my muscles. Daddy, look at you—you're a'rainin' in the face. Are you all right?'

"'Uh-uh,' I said. 'Those ain't no muscles, Baby. That had to be something else. I ain't never in my life felt no muscles like them.'

"'That's because, Daddy, you ain't never in your life had a woman like me,' Joyce says, just a'laughin' at me while I must've been lookin' like I was still scared to death.

"'OK, then, I wanna see 'em! Baby, we ain't doin' nothin' until I make sure,' I said to Joyce, tiptoeing slowly back over to where she was lying and tryin' to peek between her legs like an idiot."

The whole tier was cracking up, even some guards.

"You want to know something?" said Herbert, waiting for things to quiet down. "Check: y'all don't know how stupid I felt to have lost the feeling of a woman's love. But man, this prison can sure do it to you. I'm just glad as hell that Joyce took it all in stride and found it even funnier than all of you."

Herbert wrapped up his story. "The next morning when Joyce and me gets up and makes us some breakfast, she gets to eyeballing me from across the table, like something is wrong. Now, I can tell Joyce is trying to drink her coffee, but man, every time she brings that cup to her lips, she gets to giggling. For two whole days, that's all that woman did was giggle. She laughed so hard that all she had to do was look at me and the tears would stream down her face."

FUNNY HOW TIME FLIES

"Say, bunchy, where did you get that nice watch?" I asked. A group of us were standing along the fence of the prison exercise yard one very cold morning. "Let me check it out."

"That youngster they call Detroit gave it to me before he booked home," Bunchy said.

"Is that right?"

"Yeah, man, he looked out for the old-timer and gave me this watch."

"Well," said Motown, looking down at Bunchy's watch, "it sure looks a helluva lot better than that old raggedy Mickey Mouse Timex you had. Man, do y'all know when I first came to this joint, eleven years ago, Bunchy had that same old-ass Timex on. That watch had to be fifty years old."

"Nah, it wasn't that old," said Bunchy.

"Yeah, I'm hip," I said. "He had it on when I first met him too, and that was ten or eleven years back. Damn, Bunchy, it's about time you finally got something new around your wrist, and it's one of those quartzes, too."

"All I need now," Bunchy said, "is a battery. That young dude Gus 'posed to bring me one in a few minutes."

"Who is Gus?" I asked.

"You know Gus, that youngster that just came in on a parole violation, the one that you guys be callin' my son, that skinny dude that squeeeak when he talk and always lookin' scared."

"Oh, him," I said. "Here he comes now." We all turned and looked across the exercise yard.

"Hey, Gus," Bunchy called. "You got that battery, huh?"

"Yeah, man. Here it is."

"Right on," said Bunchy. "I appreciate it."

"No problem. I'll holler at you later. I got to go rap to a few people."

"Man," said Bunchy, looking down at his watch. "Now how do I 'posed to put this damn little battery in?"

"That's easy," I said. "Let me see your watch. You got to open the back up like this, I think."

"You think! What do you mean, you think? Please don't mess off my watch, Jay, OK?"

"Man, I ain't. You got to open it up like this here. You see now, it's open," I said.

"Jay," Motown broke in, "let me do it. I can tell you don't know what the hell you're doin'."

"Here." I handed it to him. "Show us then. Show us how it's done."

"OK, give me the battery," Motown said. "This is what you do. You take this little tiny battery—damn, which is the upside of this thing?"

"Man, you don't know what the hell you're doing either," I said. "Just let me see it again; I'll fix it."

"Yeah, I do," Motown insisted. "Just hold on, just give me a minute with it."

"Motown, you're forcing it. You don't 'posed to be forcing it like that."

"I'm not forcing it."

"Yeah, you are, you're putting the damn thing in wrong. You're gonna break the damn thing!"

"There, there, it's in." Motown showed us the battery in the watch. "You see, I told y'all I knew what I was doing."

"Man, it's probably broken," I said.

"Nah, it's not broken. Man, it's gonna work. Now all I have

to do is place this seal back on. Now, you see," Motown said, "it should be working."

"Let me have my watch," said Bunchy. "I know it's fuck' up now. You see," he said, holding the watch up to his ear, "I told you it's fuck' up. Man, I can't hear shit. It ain't tickin'. I can't hear it tickin'. Y'all done fuck' up my damn watch."

"Not me, no way. That wasn't me," I said. "Motown, he messed it up. I told you he would. Let me check it." I held the watch up to my ear. "Yep, you're right. It ain't tickin'. I can't hear nothin'. Motown, you done broke Bunchy's new watch."

"Ah, man, that's bullshit. I didn't break it. That battery must not be any good. Let me see it." I handed him the watch. "Yeah, that battery must be dead," said Motown, "because I can't hear it tickin' either."

"Just give me back the damn watch," Bunchy said. "I should've known y'all didn't know what the hell you were doin'. Shit, y'all been in this penitentiary just as long as I have and don't know nothin' about all this new high-tech shit."

"Man," Motown pleaded, "it's the battery. That battery must be dead. You should ask that youngster Gus if that battery is dead or not."

"Hey—hey, Gus!" Bunchy hollered angrily across the exercise yard. "Bring your goddamn young ass over here. Get over here, dude."

Motown and I chuckled.

"Yeah, what's up?" Gus asked, looking frightened.

"Man, did you give me a dead battery?"

"Nah, Bunchy, that's a brand-new battery. I just got that battery about a week ago. It works, Bunchy."

"Well, somethin' must be wrong with it, because my watch ain't tickin'. I can't hear my watch tickin', and I know it isn't my watch that's fuck' up."

Gus turned to the rest of us and began laughing.

"What's so funny? Is there somethin' funny?" Bunchy asked angrily.

"Nah, man, it really ain't funny," said Gus, "but man, man . . ."

"Man, hell," said Motown. "Just say it, dude! What's up?"

"Well, it's a thing like this," said Gus. "Y'all been over here putting that watch to y'all ears, trying to see if the watch is working, right? Well, man, nowadays, they don't make watches that makes tickin' sounds. It's working! They just don't make noise no more," he said, falling to his knees laughing.

"Huh?"

"Say what?"

"Is that right?"

All of us stared, mouths open, at Gus lying on the ground, laughing.

MOURNING
EXERCISE

RECIPE FOR PRISON PRUNO

Take ten peeled oranges,
Jarvis Masters, it is the judgment and sentence of this court,
one 8 oz. bowl of fruit cocktail,
that the charged information was true,
squeeze the fruit into a small plastic bag,
and the jury having previously, on said date,
and put the juice along with the mash inside,
found that the penalty shall be death,
add 16 oz. of water and seal the bag tightly.
and this Court having, on August 20, 1991,
Place the bag into your sink,
denied your motion for a new trial,
and heat it with hot running water for 15 minutes.
it is the order of this Court that you suffer death,
wrap towels around the bag to keep it warm for fermentation.
said penalty to be inflicted within the walls of San Quentin,
Stash the bag in your cell undisturbed for 48 hours.
at which place you shall be put to death,
When the time has elapsed,
in the manner prescribed by law,
add 40 to 60 cubes of white sugar,
the date later to be fixed by the Court in warrant of execution.
six teaspoons of ketchup,
You are remanded to the custody of the warden of San Quentin,
then heat again for 30 minutes,
to be held by him pending final

secure the bag as done before,

determination of your appeal.

then stash the bag undisturbed again for 72 hours.

It is so ordered.

Reheat daily for 15 minutes.

In witness whereof,

After 72 hours,

I have hereon set my hand as Judge of this Superior Court,

with a spoon, skim off the mash,

and I have caused the seal of this Court to be affixed thereto.

pour the remaining portion into two 18 oz. cups.

May God have mercy on your soul.

When I first got charged with murder, it seemed unreal to me. A woman judge was assigned to the case, and I remember having had a woman judge the first time I was taken away from my mother. Twenty years ago I stood in a courtroom while they tried to figure out what to do with me, where I should live. I was a ward of the state, and they told me they wanted to protect me. And now I was in the same kind of room, with dim buzzing lights, and they were figuring out how to try me and maybe kill me. That night I reflected a lot on the difference.

As other people started to do their job of finding a way to save my life, I joined the crusade. I had never cooperated before. But for the first time ever, I was determined to find out what was going on with me. I didn't want to justify the things I had done, and I wasn't cooperating now just to save my skin. Wanting to know the facts about myself made me take my life seriously for the first time. I had always lived with death, in the street, in prison, and I understood what leads people to prison. But I didn't understand Jarvis.

Looking back, I realize that it wasn't rage that motivated me, though I hid behind anger to avoid certain truths about my life. I remember once walking down the street, when I came across a tree growing in the pavement of a parking lot between cars. My first reaction was to look at it, study it, wonder. I thought, "How is this possible?" But I wasn't in school, I'd never learn these things. I smashed the little tree because I knew I'd never go to school. There was no room for wonder in my life.

SCARS

I remember the first time I really noticed the scars on the bodies of my fellow prisoners. I was outside on a maximum-custody exercise yard. I stood along the fence, praising the air the yard gave my lungs that my prison cell didn't. I wasn't in a rush to pick up a basketball or do anything. I just stood in my own silence.

I looked at the other prisoners, playing basketball or handball, showering, talking to one another. I saw the inmates I felt closest to, John, Pete, and David, lifting weights. I noticed the amazing similarity of the whiplike scars on their bare skin, shining with sweat from pumping iron in the hot sun.

A deep sadness came over me as I watched these powerful men lift hundreds of pounds of weights over their heads. I looked around the yard and made the gruesome discovery that everyone else had the same deep gashes—behind their legs, on their backs, all over their ribs—evidence of the violence in our lives.

Here were America's lost children—surviving in rage and in refuge from society. I was certain that many of their crimes could be traced to the horrible violence done to them as children.

The histories of all of us in San Quentin were so similar it was as if we had the same parents. Though I was a trusted comrade of most of these inmates, and to a few of them I was their only family, normally I wouldn't dare intrude on their private pain. Even so, I made up my mind that I would bring John, Pete, and David together to talk about their scars. These men had probably never spoken openly of their terrible childhood experiences. I doubted that any of them would ever have used the word "abuse." They looked hardened to the core, standing around the weight-lifting bench, proud of their bodies and the images they projected.

It occurred to me, as I approached them, that such a posture of pride symbolized the battles they had "made their bones" with. This was prison talk for "proved their manhood." At one time I had been hardened as well and had made my own denials. The difficulty I would have in speaking with them would be interpreting the prison language we all used when talking about our pasts. Shucking and jiving was the way we covered up sensitive matters.

John was a twenty-eight-year-old bulky man serving twenty-five to life for murder. I had met him when we were both in youth homes in southern California. We were only eleven years old. Throughout the years, we traveled together through the juvenile system until the penitentiary became our final stop.

When I asked him about the scars on his face he said, "They came from kickin' ass and, in the process, getting my ass kicked, which was rare."

John explained that his father had loved him enough to teach him how to fight when he was only five years old. He learned from the beatings he got. In a sense, he said, he grew up with a loving fear of his father. He pointed to a nasty scar on his upper shoulder. Laughing, he told us that his father had hit him with a steel rod when he tried to protect his mother from being beaten.

Most of us had seen this scar but had never had the nerve to ask about it. As we stared at it, John seemed ashamed. Avoiding our eyes, he mumbled a few words before showing us his many other scars. He could remember every detail surrounding the violent events that had produced them. I realized that these experiences haunted him. Yet as he went on talking, he became increasingly rational. He had spent more than half his life in one institutional setting or another, and as a result he projected a very cold and fearsome, almost boastful smile. He wanted nothing of what he shared with us to be interpreted, even remotely, as child abuse.

This was especially apparent when he showed us a gash on his back that was partially hidden by a dragon tattoo. It was a hideous scar—something I would have imagined finding on a slave who had been whipped. John motioned me closer and said, "Rub your finger down the dragon's spine." I felt what seemed like thick, tight string that moved like a worm beneath his skin.

"Damn, John, what in the hell happened to you?" I asked.

There was something in the way I questioned him that made John laugh, and the others joined in. He explained that when he was nine his father chased him with a cord. John ran under a bed, grabbed the springs, and held on as his father pulled him by the legs, striking his back repeatedly with the cord until he fell unconscious. He woke up later with a deep flesh wound. John, smiling coldly, joked that that was the last time he ever ran from his father.

David and Pete recounted similar childhood experiences. Their stories said much about how all of us had come to be in one of the worst prisons in the country. Most prisoners who were abused as children were taken from their natural parents at a very early age and placed in foster homes, youth homes, or juvenile halls for protection, where they acquired even more scars. Later in their lives prisons provided the same kind of painful refuge. It is terrifying to realize that a large percentage of prisoners will eventually reenter society, father children, and perpetuate what happened to them.

Throughout my many years of institutionalization, I, like so many of these men, unconsciously took refuge behind prison walls. Not until I read a series of books for adults who had been abused as children did I become committed to the process of examining my own childhood. I began to unravel the reasons I had always just expected to go from one youth institution to the next. I never really tried to stay out of these places, and neither did my friends.

That day I spoke openly to my friends about my physical and mental abuse as a child. I told them that I had been neglected and then abandoned by my parents, heroin addicts, when I was very young. I was beaten and whipped by my stepfather. My mother left me and my sisters alone for days with our newborn twin brother and sister when I was only four years old. The baby boy died a crib death, and I always believed it was my fault, since I had been made responsible for him. I spoke to them of the pain I had carried through more than a dozen institutions, pain I could never face. And I explained how all of these events ultimately trapped me in a pattern of lashing out against everything.

But these men could not think of their own experiences as abuse. What I had told them seemed to sadden them, perhaps because I had embraced a hidden truth that they could not. They avoided making the connection between my experiences and theirs. It was as if they felt I had suffered more than they. That wasn't true. What they heard was their own unspoken words.

Eventually, we all fell silent around the weight-lifting bench, staring across the yard at the other men exercising.

John and I spoke again privately later. "You know something?" he said. "The day I got used to getting beaten by my father and by the counselors in all those group homes was the day I knew nothing would ever hurt me again. Everything I thought could hurt me I saw as a game. I had nothing to lose and just about everything to gain. A prison cell will always be here for me."

John was speaking for most of the men I had met in prison. Secretly, we like it here. This place welcomes a man who is full of rage and violence. He is not abnormal here, not different. Prison life is an extension of his inner life.

Finally, I confided to John that I wished I had been with my mother when she died.

"Hey, didn't you say she neglected you?" he asked.

John was right, she had neglected me, but am I to neglect myself as well by denying that I wished I'd been with her when she died, that I still love her?

Me and my sisters lived in the same room. My mother used to go out at night and come back early in the morning and sleep all day. We'd brush her hair and comfort her while she slept. We took care of ourselves while she was away. I was about four, Charlene was six, Bertie was three, and Carlette was just a baby.

One night, my mother came rushing in, telling us to pack our stuff, she was in a world of trouble. We spent five, six minutes packing, the baby was crying, it was very chaotic. I remember my mother grabbing me, jerking me, looking at me in the face and shaking me, telling me, "If anything happens to me, you take care of your sisters."

The next thing I know, the door bangs open, I hear a man say, "Where are you, bitch? I'm gonna kill you and your kids!"

My mother pushes us all under the bed, in a particular order, with me on the outside.

"Where are those kids?" he yells.

My mother runs out panicked. I'd never seen her so panicked, with sweat dripping from her face. She runs out into the next room and they start fighting. I could hear him pounding her flesh. Boom! Boom! Boom! I winced every time she got hit. My sisters and I jerked with every strike, like we were being hit ourselves. The table was knocked over, chairs were falling, pictures coming off the walls, the whole house was rumbling. When my mother stopped crying, we could still hear her being hit.

Then our door kicks open and I see these shoes. These shoes were the scariest thing I ever saw in my life. I remember looking up to try to see who it was. To this day, whenever I get scared my eyes still go up into my head like they did that day.

As he comes in, he's yelling, "Where you motherfuckin' kids at? I'm gonna kill you, too!"

He takes three steps into the bedroom, and I remember those three steps. As soon as he puts his foot down that third time, here comes my mother. She jumps on his back and starts pounding away at him, screaming, "You ain't gonna kill my kids!"

They fall into the next room. The kitchen dishes go flying. I could hear him kicking her, stomping on her. I could hear her yelling, "Help! Please, no!"

She fell silent and I could hear him still pounding her. We were all frozen with fear. My sister Bertie had some kind of seizure. The pounding went on and on and on.

When it finally stopped, I remember thinking, "Momma told me to stay here and not move." It was a hard decision for me to stay there under the bed. My mother said I was the man of the house. I didn't know whether I should stay there to protect my sisters or not.

I fell asleep. It was a nervous sleep. Then I woke up and saw what looked like a monster crawling into the room. Her lip was dragging all the way down. Her eyes, you couldn't even see them. Blood was pouring out of her face. I remember her earrings.

My mother was just a few feet away from us. Using all the strength she had left, she picked her head up as high as she could and reached for us with her hand. She fell hard, hitting her head on the floor.

Charlene and I crawled out from under the bed. I sat on the floor, holding my mother's head in my lap. My tiny hands tried to wipe the blood away from her face, but it kept pouring out.

Charlene went and got a towel and it got soaked with blood immediately. We just couldn't stop it. We started to panic. Charlene and I looked up at each other at the same time and just starting screaming. That woke my mother up; her eyes opened a little. She gripped my hand real, real tight, and then she smiled as if to say we were all right and still together.

Charlene just fell on her, hugging her. I kept screaming and some white woman, a neighbor, came in and called the ambulance.

■ ■ ■

My mother died while I was here in prison, before I could spend much time with her. It was at a point when I finally had the strength to talk to her about the experiences that had led to my long separation from her as a child. The greatest moment I could have given her would have been to tell her that, through it all, I loved her.

Many people think of her as someone I'm not supposed to love, a woman who abandoned and neglected me. But my own memory of her isn't tainted that way. When I was young, I felt extremely sad for her, and later I saw her as a victim.

My last memory of the two of us together is of watching my mother hold her newborn grandchild for the first time. She sat on the couch rocking little Donta, her eyes filled with love and memories of all of us. Then she wept, singing one of her favorite songs. It was a song by Billie Holiday. As a child, I had heard her sing the same lyrics: "Mama may have, Papa may have, but God bless the child who's got his own . . . who's got his own."

MOURNING EXERCISE

The day was just getting started when I went out to the exercise yard. I was one of the last prisoners to be let out, so I knew I wouldn't have a chance to play basketball. The teams would have already been picked, and they would go on playing with each other until the high-tower buzzer indicated that our three hours of exercise time were up.

It was exhilarating to be outside after three hot summer days cooped up in my single-man cell. My mood was expansive as I wandered about, talking to my fellow prisoners. Other men in the yard were lifting weights and gambling around the game table for push-ups.

An excellent day, I thought, to just hang out and take in some sun. I took off my T-shirt and leaned against the fence, watching everyone from the corner of the yard. There were the cheaters like Ace and Slick on the basketball court, and Billy and Sonny on the handball court. They were incredibly skillful. Many years of playing together had fine-tuned them like naturals. I watched them win game after game under the burning sun.

I was the first to see the prison chaplain approach the fence. The yard suddenly fell silent. I held my breath, hoping he wasn't headed my way. Most of us never saw the prison chaplain unless it was Christmas or we were about to receive some very bad news.

The chaplain walked along the fence, staring through his wire-frame glasses. He seemed like a messenger of death. I wanted to turn away and pretend I'd never seen this man of the cloth before. But, like so many of my fellow prisoners, I had: this very priest had brought me the news of the sudden deaths of my mother, brother, and sister.

He pressed his hands against the fence, his eyes searching intently for someone in the yard. I had nothing—no basketball to bounce, no handball to hit, no weights to lift—to distract me from my inner pleading, "Not me again!"

First relief, then sadness swept over me when I saw the chaplain trying to get Freddie's attention on the basketball court. "Hey, Freddie," he said. "Buddy, I have a bit of bad news for you. I need to speak to you—just for a minute, OK?" But Freddie only played harder. I watched fear pinch his eyes as he tried to concentrate. The other players upped the pace of the game as if to shield him from the chaplain's voice. This was their way of supporting their friend for as long as he needed to deny that the chaplain's news was for him.

I had known Freddie for many years in San Quentin. We were always on the same basketball team. Like me, he was thirty-two, but six foot, bulky and powerful, stronger than I was. He was serving a fifty-year-to-life sentence and could easily bench-press the heaviest bar, 450 pounds. No one else on the yard could lift as much as he could.

The chaplain remained poised at the fence, waiting patiently. I pondered the many phone calls he had received over the years from the outside world, informing him whose mother, son, or daughter had died. He had come to know that many prisoners are capable of shedding their hardened images, to break down and cry like any other human being.

I looked at Freddie. Neither his mind nor physical skills could forestall the tragedy awaiting him. He played aggressively, like a stranger to his teammates. But even they began to acknowledge what he had to do, and finally so did Freddie.

He walked over to the fence, and he and the chaplain stood

together for a minute or two. Then Freddie stepped back, a slight smile on his face, and the basketball game resumed. I was shocked. The Freddie I knew couldn't possibly take this so well. The noise level on the yard picked up again.

Several minutes later Freddie glanced up at the two guardsmen in the gun tower. I didn't make much of it, until he turned and I could see that his eyes were filled with tears, just as tears had filled my own world when members of my family had died. He was fighting hard to stay strong, to keep the pain from showing, to resist his desire to cry in front of us, whose tears he had never seen.

Freddie didn't let himself cry. Instead, rage began rolling through him like a thunder cloud about to burst. His fists tightened and his body shook violently. "Damn, he's going to explode!" I thought.

Rattler, Ace, and Slick, who were standing on the court with him, had overheard the chaplain tell him his grandmother, his only family, had died from a heart attack. They realized that he was losing it, spinning off the scales of his sanity. They approached him, like courageous swimmers, venturing into the depths of the ocean to save a drowning comrade who had begun to panic.

Rattler reached his hand out to Freddie, only to be answered with blows to his head. The tower guardsmen fired two warning shots in the air. "Freeze!" they ordered, but Freddie kept swinging violently at his friends. His rage was directed not against them, but against his own will to survive.

As his friends tried to back off, Freddie lunged at them, pulling them down hard onto the asphalt. The guardsmen yelled another warning before pointing their rifles and firing into the yard. Pow! Pow! . . . Pow! Pow! . . . Pow! The bullets punched deep holes into the asphalt, only inches away from the men scuffling on the ground. Pow! Pow!

"Don't shoot!" hollered Rattler. "Man, don't shoot! Can't you see there's something wrong with him?"

"Back away from him! Get off him!" a guard barked from the gun tower. The rifles were still pointed down; their next shots would not be aimed to miss.

"Hell, no!" shouted Rattler.

They had finally pinned Freddie to the ground and were struggling to keep him there.

"Man, can't you see something's wrong with him?" Rattler screamed, tears pouring down his face. "Can't you see he needs help? Hell, just shoot us, kill us all!"

Ace and Slick began to sob too as they held Freddie. They were suddenly holding each other, not as hardened prisoners, but simply as human beings. The entire exercise yard, all fifty or more of us, stared in amazement.

It was as humans first and men second that we all, including Freddie, returned to our cells that day.

DREAM

I slipped into a dream after watching the nightly news on television in the summer of 1992, the summer when Californians braced themselves for their first state execution in more than twenty-seven years.

I was with close friends on the deck of a giant boat, surrounded by miles of ocean. As we enjoyed ourselves in the blazing sun, a crew of men worked on some diving equipment, making it ready for us. We all wanted to explore the ocean depths and the many beautiful species inhabiting this great sea.

On the side of the boat was a small single-man diving bell, and someone was testing its system of communication with the main boat. We all mingled around the bell, chatting about how expensive it must have been.

The diving bell was green and shaped like a capsule or a miniature submarine. It had two small windows on each side and one thick chamber door in front. Attached to the top was a single fat rubber tube. It seemed to be suspended by an electronic chain belt, and a remote-control crane moved it from side to side.

I was the first to go inside. The heavy chamber door slammed shut, sealing me in, and I sat there not knowing what to expect. I heard the clanking sounds of the crane lifting the diving bell off the boat and the chain belt lowering it slowly onto the surface of the water.

I peered out the window as the bell submerged into the sea. I could see millions of tiny brilliant bubbles all around me. They were magnificent. They sparkled, then vanished, and the ocean transformed into a beautiful aquarium filled with fish swimming around the bell. There were thousands of them, of all colors and sizes, their tails swaying gracefully right before my eyes. I think we smiled at each other.

As I plunged deeper into this marvelous hidden world, I felt I was being swallowed into the vast throat of Mother Earth, and the many forms I was gazing at were like thousands of microscopic cells traveling throughout this vast body of life.

Then suddenly my mind sobered, and I became frightened. Where was I? As I spiraled down into this sea that had turned to night, its inhabitants began to terrify me.

My heart started to pound like a drum against my chest; I felt claustrophobic and short of breath. I grabbed the microphone above me and called out for help. But there was no reply—no human being heard me as I descended deeper into the black hole of the sea. "Where are my friends?" I wondered, and panicked all the more now that I was lost from all of them.

My throat started to swell, and I staggered out of my seat. I had no balance and lost my sight, until an awful vision began to unfold. Monstrous faces appeared, as if summoned to witness my fate in this inescapable chamber of hell. I tried desperately to fight them off, but I couldn't breathe. "Help me . . . Lord God," I gasped. "Help me, O Buddha! O Allah! O Jehovah! O Krishna!" I pleaded, knowing with certainty that I was going to die.

Finally I collapsed onto the cold floor, choking on the dead, toxic air. For a while I lay in a fetal position, hugging my knees tightly. Then I began to thrash around, suffocating, vomiting, my body jerking. The pain was so great that my fingers stiffened into prying forks, and my nails scraped the floor, snagging threads of green paint.

After a while, I just lay there, not moving. I fell in and out of consciousness, my mind and body giving up on life—wishing only that the floor beneath me could somehow cushion this dying body.

While conscious, I could see my wonderful friends above me, on the huge boat. We stared at each other, aware that these would be our last moments together. Some of them tried to reassure me, "It'll be all right . . . it'll be all right." Others said, "Take care, we love you, Jarvis." They all began to cry, watching me slowly inhale my last deep breath. I held it in, a sign to them that I was saying goodbye.

When I woke up, I was hyperventilating and my body was drenched. I was bleeding from scratches I had carved into my own flesh.

"What a nightmare!" I thought. But then I realized something even worse: I had awakened again on death row.

I open my palms to the sky,
surrendering to my human hopelessness,
that it doesn't despair me.
For life needs no more,
no more despair, I pray.

JUSTICE MARSHALL RESIGNS

It was four o'clock, a hot day in the Adjustment Center, when my friend Vernon broke the silence.

"Man, did you hear what they just said on the news?" he yelled through his cell bars. "Justice Marshall of the U.S. Supreme Court just resign'. It's on Channel Five right now."

Everyone in the range of Vernon's voice started flipping through their television channels. Pete yelled that it was also on Channel Seven.

"It's on Channel Four, too," Louis called out.

"What's going on?" asked Hector, who didn't have a TV.

"Man, they have special news bulletins on all the stations," Vernon said. "Justice Marshall just sent in his resignation to President Bush. Those of us on the row is washed up now. They said he's resigning due to old age, but that's bullshit. It's because he don't want to be party to what he can't stop—not only on the death penalty, but on abortion, civil rights, and all sorts of other rulings that this conservative court will be handing down."

"Yeah, I think you're right, Vernon. Hey, Paul," I called down the tier. "What do you think?"

"Jarvis, I'm just tripping on it all. I mean, Marshall was a great man, you know? Did any of you ever watch that documentary about him on the PBS station? He was a civil rights lawyer in the early fifties, working for the NAACP, and he argued that 1954 case of Brown versus Board of Education. He was in the forefront of civil rights. Now that he won't be on the Supreme Court anymore, I don't think America will ever be the same."

"Hey, do you think Bush will accept Marshall's resignation?" Louie asked.

"Hell, yeah."

"Shit, yeah."

"Hell, yes."

"Fuckin' right."

The tier fell into troubled silence. We were all absorbed in our thoughts—our gut feelings as to what Marshall's resignation meant to each of us. The moment had grabbed our attention as if we'd heard a great bomb whistling down on us.

Finally Hector said, "It's only a matter of time."

"He read my mind," I thought.

"Man, that's just what I was thinking," Louie said.

"Shit, that's what we were all thinking," added Vernon.

Just then the evening food cart appeared. "Chow time," the guards yelled, heading toward the back end of the tier. When they got to my cell, one of them asked, "You want anything? No one seem' to be hungry today."

"No, I'm not hungry myself," I said. "Just give mine to someone else."

"You sure?" he said.

"Yeah, I'm sure."

"OK, then. I just have to take all this food back to the kitchen." I watched the guard wheel the cart back down the tier.

BRYAN

For hours San Quentin had not existed. There were only a few pages left, and I hadn't put the book down since the first page. I had escaped all evening.

Glancing at my watch, I was startled to see it was after two o'clock. I eased from my bunk and stretched before moving three steps to the front of the cell. In a daze, my hands resting on the cell bars, I looked out the window opposite my cell. "How peaceful it is," I thought, gazing into the windless, soft stillness of the night.

Suddenly, like a horror film screened on the prison wall, a painful memory came alive, replaying an autumn night seven years before, a night when I had also stayed awake this late.

On that night I had just lit my last cigarette when I thought I heard Bryan's voice, whispering to me from the next cell. It was dark and quiet in the Adjustment Center. The guards had just made their rounds and left the tier.

Bryan called out softly, "Hey, Jarvis, are you awake down there? Are you, man? What are you doing?"

"Nothing much, just getting ready to turn in. What's up?" I asked.

Seconds went by. Bryan moved closer to the front of his cell. He squatted down and began talking in a low tone so that only I could hear him.

"You know something, Jay? I never thought it would come to this."

"What's that?" I asked.

"Prison, man, prison," said Bryan. "I just realized tonight

that I'm never getting out of here. This is it for me. My world ends here. San Quentin!"

Bryan was a small, thin kid whose youthful wild streak and childlike voice had earned him the prison nickname "Youngster."

"Damn," said Bryan. "I need a cigarette. I haven't smoked one in two years, but I can use one right now. Do you have a spare smoke?"

"Give me a minute," I said quietly, reaching for an unopened pack. "Do you have a fishline over there?"

"No, but I'll make one."

I heard Bryan tearing thin strips from a bed sheet. The sound was loud in the quiet building.

"Hey, I'm only in the cell next to you. You don't need so much line," I joked.

"As long as I'm making a fishline," said Bryan, "I may as well make it long enough to reach farther down the tier."

Minutes went by. Finally Bryan threw his line in front of my cell. I took two cigarettes, lit one for myself, and tied the other to Bryan's line. Bryan pulled it in.

"What time is it?" Bryan asked.

"Almost three o'clock," I answered, squatting at the front of my cell, puffing on a cigarette, looking into the quiet night.

I knew the youngster was frightened. Bryan was only sixteen years old when he left the violence of the gang turfs to serve a life sentence for the murder of another youth. He had been tried as an adult. Now he understood that for the rest of his life he would live confined within a state penitentiary.

"Jay," Bryan said, "the night I killed that dude in the park, it was either him or me. This prison makes me wish that it was me dead and him in this cell. Damn this cell. I don't care if they kill me tomorrow."

I felt a deep sadness for my friend. I knew that Bryan's sentence had just begun, while my own had started many years earlier. I remembered how I had felt when the reality of prison had hit me—under cover of darkness, in the night silence of prisoner loneliness.

Though I couldn't see Bryan, I knew that a young man was staring into the shadows of his inner pain.

Bryan didn't say anything more, so I called out, "Youngster? Are you awake down there? I know you haven't gone to sleep on me. Hey, Youngster. I know you can hear me. What are you doing?"

There was no response. Not wanting to violate the quiet airspace of the other prisoners, I said nothing else. But I decided to stay awake in case Bryan needed to talk.

Lying on my bunk looking out on the tier, I fought to keep my eyes open. As tired as I was, I believed I had real reasons for staying awake. The cold air helped. I watched a mouse come out from hiding as the night grew even quieter. Suddenly, I heard a sound. It seemed to come from the broken windows across the tier—a strong shift of wind, I thought. I looked at my watch and realized I had dozed off. It was close to six o'clock. I climbed from my bunk and went to the sink to wash my face.

Toilets began flushing in nearby cells. I heard the jingling of guards' keys and a food cart being wheeled onto the tier. I wondered at which end of the tier the guards would start serving morning chow.

I called cheerfully to Bryan, "Hey, Youngster, rise and shine. It's time to get up!"

Suddenly a guard's whistle shrilled like a scream of panic. I ran to the back of my cell and crouched down by the sink, waiting to hear something that would tell me what was going on.

Within seconds a guard cried at the top of his lungs, "Man down! Man down! We have a man down!"

"What cell?" yelled the guard stationed off the tier. "What's going on . . . What do you have down there?"

"Jesus," muttered the first guard, and then he shouted, "Suicide. We have a suicide in cell sixty-five."

Then I heard guards storming onto the tier toward my cell.

I called out, "Hey, Bry—" then caught myself. "That's Bryan's cell," I thought. "Damn, Bryan's in number sixty-five."

I inched to the front of the cell, afraid that I might see the guards standing at my friend's cell. "Nah, not Bryan," I prayed. But as I looked out and saw the guards, tears rained from my eyes.

The guards were in riot gear, their batons drawn, waiting for Bryan's cell to come open. The guard controlling the bar gates hollered down the line, "Stand clear! Number sixty-five is opening! Opening sixty-five!"

As the bars were pulled back, guards swarmed into the cell. I heard them debating. "Let's cut him down." "No, we can't cut him down until medical staff arrives."

An uproar began as prisoners all over the tier yelled in rage, "Cut him down! Cut him down! Cut him down!"

I stood with my bare back pressed against the wall that had separated me from Bryan all night. My exhausted mind started replaying our conversation. If only I had stayed awake, I might have helped my friend.

I stared up at the ceiling, covering my ears, trying not to hear, picturing Bryan hanging from the air vent on the back wall of his cell—dead.

When I looked out of the cell again, Bryan's body was on a gurney, surrounded by guards; the tier was silent. A medic told

a guard, "He's a little cold . . . he's been dead quite some time."
I could see Bryan's eyes. One was closed, the other staring up
toward his forehead. Thin braided strips of sheet were wrapped
tightly around his neck. The ends hung down to the floor.

Suddenly a bright light flashed on me, shocking me out of my
memory of Bryan seven years earlier. It was a guard's flashlight.

"You're still awake," the guard said, prowling down the tier.

I nodded. I turned from the bars and sat on the bunk, staring
at the wall. For the hundredth time I wondered what I should
have said to Bryan. I imagined pleading with him.

"Bryan, I know what you're feeling. But all of life is precious—
even yours in prison. No matter how difficult your life seems
tonight, no matter how isolated you feel, you're not alone. There
are so many babies dying, homeless people in the streets, millions of people starving. There is so much suffering, a lot worse
than yours. Sometimes we have to challenge ourselves to survive. I love you, dude. Don't kill yourself . . . Don't kill yourself."

I almost believed that if I had said all this, Bryan would still
be alive. I turned and watched the light of morning appear in the
window. I tried to relax my mind.

Suddenly something dawned on me. I couldn't have stopped
Bryan from taking his life. How could I have? Maybe there were
words that would have saved him, but at that time I hadn't found
them.

It's become so hard for me to live in this prison culture while no longer feeling a part of it. I see clearly now why most prisoners are afraid to deal with their rage and hatred, because if they did, the prison environment would become unbearable. It seems as though the more I shed the part of me that once saw prison as an extension of my inner life, the more often I go back to my old habit of chain smoking and staring through my cell bars late at night, trying to keep myself together.

I don't fear death most of the time, but what I do fear all the time is how I'm going to die. It has been decreed that I be put in a chamber that will gas the breath out of me, while people watch, write, and sketch me strapped in a chair, fighting for my life. It will be society's statement that something inhuman has been executed. When I think about the fact that society, a nation, has sentenced me to death, all I can do is turn inside myself, to the place in my heart that wants so desperately to feel human, still connected to this world, as if I have a purpose. But then the next day, a prisoner will ask me to write a letter for him because he doesn't know how to write, and I'll say sure, grateful to him for giving me another reason to be at peace.

Sometimes I feel so confused, worried, and troubled, I just want to hate things. For most of my life, I pretended to know how to hate—I used the word a lot. But I never felt the hate that could be justified by all the bullshit I've suffered.

My stepfather tried to teach me how to hate as a child. He said it was for my own protection. He used to lock me between his legs and slap me on the head and face until rage filled my body. He'd say, "Get mad . . . fight, son . . . fight," and I would. Afterward, I'd be in pain, though more saddened for him. Once I contemplated stabbing him with a kitchen knife as he slept, but I couldn't do it.

In the same way, I can't hate the people who sentenced me to death or the judge who said I should never have been born.

Sometimes I can't escape the pressure tightening around my brain. I get so that I don't want or can't keep the nasty prison food in my stomach. I have to run to my TV or radio not to hear myself think, to divert my attention from everything around me: this prison, death row, the cold feeling of being trapped in total isolation.

O. J.

"Hey, check out the news on Channel Seven!" Satchmo shouted through his cell bars, his voice echoing down the tier. "Man, this is the craziest stuff I've ever seen," he said with disgust.

I could hear people from one end of the tier to the next moving to turn their televisions on, flipping through their channels. We were curious about what brought Satchmo out of his usual regimented silence.

I quickly turned on my television, but failed to see anything that seemed important enough to have excited Satchmo, who we all knew was only into international issues and political stuff. As he was quick to remind anyone, he was a revolutionary, pro-IRA, pro-Kadafi, pro-Hussein, pro-Castro, pro anything in opposition to the United States.

"Hey, Jarvis," my neighbor Percy called over to me. "Man, what's up? It's just a bunch of kids with their parents buyin' Halloween costumes on Seven."

"Yeah, I know," I said, thinking that maybe Satchmo had made a mistake.

"That's it!" hollered Satchmo. "Check it out. Man, these fools are selling O. J. Simpson Halloween costumes, bloody knife and all. See that kid in the background, you see what he got on?"

"Wow! Look at that shit, Jarvis!" Percy exclaimed.

I spotted a small boy, who looked about eight or nine, wearing an O. J. Simpson mask, a bloody number thirty-two football jersey, a black glove, and holding a rubber knife.

"Damn!" I half whispered. The news reporter was interviewing the store manager, who beamed a giant smile as he spoke proudly of the profits his store was making from the sale of the costumes. As he talked, the boy—knife held high—began chasing a little girl up and down the aisle. My stomach did a couple of flips.

"Run, O. J., run!" someone down the tier blurted out, then burst into laughter.

"Man! You's a sick bastard," said Satchmo.

"Yeah, fuck O. J. and you," another voice shouted at Satchmo. These were the two crazies at the very end of the tier. They usually seized upon any opportunity to get people's attention by acting foolishly.

I reached over and turned off my television. The news segment had left me feeling sick. For an instant, I felt truly fortunate to be on death row, soon to be dead and gone from this troubled society.

"Man, Jarvis, what do you think about all that stupid sick shit?" Percy asked.

"It's bad," I muttered. My thoughts had given me a headache. "What kind of person could imagine such a costume, let alone buy one for their own kid?"

"Shit! Hell if I know," answered Percy. "It's no wonder so many youngsters at only twelve or thirteen are committing murders these days. It's some really crazy shit going on out there."

"It's a disease," said Cochise, whose low voice could barely be heard from a few cells down. "Man, it's something that goes beyond black or white, something that thrives on the impurities of the human condition. Man, had it not been the O. J. thing, it would have simply found something else to feed on."

"What kind of disease, Cochise?" asked Little Chuck, who was in the cell next to his. At the age of nineteen, he had earned the distinction of being one of the youngest people on death row—a notoriety he didn't relish.

"Human nature . . . death . . . what else? Man, I really believe that on some primal level people find death fascinating. It's human nature to want to get as close as possible to the things we fear. Like those parents putting their kids in a bloody costume. It's pretty cannibalistic when you think about it—society feeding off itself."

"You're right, Cochise," said Percy. "It's in the culture. Hell, these kids nowadays will put a bullet in your head just to hear the sound it makes. Man, y'all remember when that lady got raped and killed and all her neighbors just watched and didn't do nothing?"

"Man, I think it runs deeper than that," said Cochise. "It makes you wonder what will be the next feeding ground."

"Hey, do y'all really want to know what kinds of vampires think of stuff like that?" Satchmo asked. His insights were always worth listening to. He'd been locked up for over twenty-five years, not all of them on death row, and was one of the few really political prisoners left in the prison system. I enjoyed hearing Satchmo. He spoke as if standing in front of thousands, his strong voice resonating throughout the tier. He had an easy, captivating manner that held your attention, even if, like me, you didn't agree with everything he said.

"It's capitalist parasites," Satchmo said. "Bloodthirsty opportunists. People who would hock their own grandmother's burial plot. This is what society is about—making that almighty dollar, even if you got to step on others to do it. A contaminated society produces contaminated children. Why, it shouldn't be no big surprise that kids are turning into miniature killing machines. Kids are born into a system that teaches that exploitation equals survival.

"Remember when y'all were growing up and had to go to church every Sunday, and you watched your mother put money in the collection basket? She was told it was for the image on the cross, a dead man. But no one who ever put money in the basket benefited from it, and they all knew how that preacher could afford to buy a shiny new car. The preacher fucked them, but they didn't want to admit it and they kept going back every Sunday. It fuckin' conditions you to keep bending over."

Satchmo stopped abruptly, leaving us dangling. He had gotten the attention of everyone on the tier, all seventeen of us, the crazies included. We all wanted him to go on, but nobody said a word. He parried our silence like a skilled swordsman, waiting for the right moment to lunge.

"But what about—" started Chuck, but Satchmo cut him off.

"Man! That store manager is just like the preacher. The only difference is what's inside the packages they're sellin'. And the urge to peep inside brings out the worst in people; when they look, they lose pieces of themselves. Shit, I have no quarrel with people like the store manager and the preacher—you teach a dog to fight and it will be prone to biting. Parasites are what they are, nothing else! On the other hand, those parents should know better."

This time Satchmo was finished. I doubt whether everyone understood him. But it wasn't his style to explain himself—he would speak uninterrupted, then draw his deep, penetrating voice back into his cell, leaving a vacuum.

No one spoke for a while. The silence finally broke when some music came floating out on the tier, as if a movie had just ended—it was a Marvin Gaye song from someone's radio, "What's Going On?"

"Hey, do y'all think O. J. is guilty?" Chuck asked.

"Man! Who cares?" responded Percy. "Shit! I don't know if

that dude is guilty or not. I don't want to know either, because that's none of my business. Hell, for all I care he can be as guilty as Ted Bundy or as innocent as the guys in that documentary—you know, *The Thin Blue Line*. Either way there's no damn excuse for society to exploit the tragedy."

"It was almost like witnessing child abuse on TV," I interjected. "The psychology is the same. It gets to me. It hurts. I wish I knew where these parents mean to take their kids with this madness, you know?"

"Hey! To San Quentin's death row!" one of the crazies hollered out. "They're bringing them right here, to take our places. It won't be long before all those toy knives turn into something mighty fine, y'all just watch . . . Chop! Chop!" He laughed uncontrollably until he started coughing.

The tier fell silent.

"What's going on, tell me, what's going on?" Marvin Gaye sang.

· · ·

In my recurrent dream I can see people gathering around to witness my execution—about a hundred of them. I'm able to identify only one person—me. I'm watching my own execution. This other "I" watches the leather belt strips tighten on my wrists and feet as I sit in a green capsule-like gas chamber. There is silent communication between us. I know I am going to be executed so that the "I" who is not will live in peace. He and I recall the years we shared, inhabiting this human body. Then when I begin to choke from the gas, the other "I" experiences his body lifting inches off the ground and floating there. He notices with amazement that he can see through his hands and through the flesh of everyone there. The only person he cannot see is me sitting in the chamber, choking and dying. Then I wake up.

FINDING FREEDOM

Night's bright stars,
celebrating life's dream;
while peace sits still.

. . .

For a long time I had been my own stranger, but everything I went through in learning how to accept myself brought me to the doorsteps of dharma, the Buddhist path.

During my death penalty trial, Melody, a private investigator working on my case, sent me books on how to meditate, how to deal with pain and suffering, how to keep my mind at rest. She had broken her ankle and was trying to keep still. She and I were both trying this meditation gig, and like me, she was confronting a lot of things in her past. She was also writing and encouraged me to do so as well.

I began to get up early to try to calm my mind so I wouldn't panic. It was as if my whole life was being displayed on a screen during the death penalty case. Things I had never realized about myself and my life were introduced to me and the jury at the same time. Questions I'd never asked my mother—like how long she'd been abused, on the street, an addict—were being asked now. Through meditation I learned to slow down and take a few deep breaths, to take everything in, not to run from the pain, but to sit with it, confront it, give it the companion it had never had. I became committed to my meditation practice.

While I was in the holding booth during the jury's deliberation on whether I should get life without parole or the death penalty, I started leafing through a Buddhist journal Melody had left there. In it was an article called "Life in Relation to Death" by a Tibetan Buddhist lama, Chagdud Tulku Rinpoche. I thought, "Wow! This is right up my alley!"

I sent a letter to the address in the journal and got a reply from a woman named Lisa, one of Rinpoche's close students, with a copy of his booklet, Life in Relation to Death. At the time, I'd gotten into some kind of trouble and was in isolated confinement, stripped down to a pair of shorts and a T-shirt, with only two blankets. In her letter, Lisa asked if I needed help. I always needed help, I still need help, and because of the help she offered, we began corresponding. Then she began to visit me and eventually brought Rinpoche to San Quentin.

When I first saw Rinpoche through the glass in the small visiting room booth, I thought, "Oh, shit, I'm in trouble now. I'm messing around with a real lama. He's from Tibet. Check him out. I bet everything he's got on is blessed."

I figured there were two ways I could introduce myself. I could greet him in an ordinary way, or I could bow. I bowed. Then he bowed. Why'd I think he wouldn't? He's been bowing all his life.

I thought, "I've been reading about lamas for the last three years and now I have a real one in front of me." I knew that all I could do was tell him exactly what I think. If I lied or shied away from him, he'd know it.

I fell in love with him for the same reasons everybody else does. His life history was my key. He had been a rebellious kid. He wasn't born with a silver spoon. He was a feisty guy who would discipline me when I needed it. He knew what he was talking about, and would say it in a way that I'd get it. He had a certain shrewdness. Compassionate ferociousness. He was a lama who ate beef jerky, got upset, and had jewels of compassion in him. The only thing he didn't do was say all this to me. I just felt it. I thought, "Here's a guy who can take me out of prison even as I remain here. He won't dress me in Buddhist garb, but accept me as I am." I knew he was a tough character.

SEEKING SILENCE

That morning I awoke at four o'clock, earlier than usual, to begin my practice of meditation. Trying not to disturb anyone sleeping in the adjacent cells, I tiptoed around in my shorts, to wash up and collect myself.

Taking a blanket off my bunk, I folded it into a small mat. The silence gave San Quentin the feel of a cemetery. I peered out the window opposite my cell into the night frost, wondering how this prison—so violent in daylight—could now seem so placidly beautiful under the heavy, watchful lightbeams of the gun towers. The hard streams of light stood adrift in the air, a far distance away.

I placed the folded blanket on the floor at the front of my cell. Such periods of silence, of breathing softly into a state of relaxation, were the most rare and wonderful experiences in all my years of incarceration. I felt calm as I sat cross-legged, facing the front of my cell. I began by naturally quieting my mind.

I had been sitting there for probably forty-five minutes before I became completely relaxed, feeling all the tension in my muscles starting to flow outward, when the silence was shattered by a loud shout— "Feed me or come fuck me up!" The voice came from a cell not far from mine.

"You motherfuckers better come feed me or fuck me up, you hear me?" the same voice roared.

"Hey, man," an irritated inmate yelled. "Why don't you shut the fuck up? Can't you see people are trying to sleep around here? They'll feed us when it's time to eat."

"Hey, why don't the both of you motherfuckers kill that god-damn noise?" a third voice spoke out loudly.

"Ah, you go fuck yourself," replied the nearby voice. "You aren't calling the shots around here, punk."

"Who you callin' a punk, punk?" the angry voice asked.

"You, you motherfucker. You don't tell me what to do. I do what the hell I want around this camp."

"So why don't you shut the fuck up then?"

"Why don't all you motherfuckers shut up?" another voice interjected angrily. "All you stupid silly mother-fuckers need to shut up and let folks sleep."

"Now, who the fuck is you?" the voice near me asked.

"Well, who the fuck is you, doing all that goddamn yelling? You better just chill out with that 'feed me' shit and rest your goddamn neck. You ain't crazy, so quit acting like you are."

"No, I'm your daddy, punk! That's who I am," shouted the nearby voice. "And you don't tell your daddy what to do, you dig? I do what the fuck I want to do, just like I told the last motherfucker."

"If you are my daddy," came the reply, "then why don't you suck my daddy's dick?"

"Sissy, you don't even have one. What you have is a cunt between your legs."

"If you see a cunt then suck on it, you bitch!"

"Your mama's a bitch, punk! That's what your mother is. She's the bitch!"

"Punk, who did you say was a bitch?"

"Whooo?" shouted the nearby voice. "Dude, your foot don't fit no limb! You ain't no owl. I said your mama's a bitch—your mother, that's who. You heard me the first time."

"OK. We'll just see who's a bitch, punk! When they rack these bar gates and all the cells come flying open, we'll just see who is the real bitch, me or you, punk."

"We'll let the gates be the bell, 'cause dude, I don't give a mad fuck. You just come out slangin' and swingin' wit' what you know best."

"Oh, I'm comin', punk," the voice said coldly. "You can bank on it."

I sat silently, listening to the enraged voices. San Quentin had come awake before I could find a meditative state, and now, as I watched the morning light appear at the window, all I could think about was how to avoid being mistakenly stabbed when all the prison cells came open.

THE DALAI LAMA HAT

It was a beautiful day, and we were all glad to be out of our cells and on the exercise yard. Everybody wanted to use the state-issued camera to take pictures. I was elected to be the cameraman.

"Hey, Jarvis, could I wear your cap for a picture to send my little girl?" Eddie asked.

"Sure! I don't see why not." I took the cap from my head and handed it to him.

"Thanks! I really appreciate it."

"You know," I said, as Eddie was fitting the cap on his head, "there's a patch blessed by the Dalai Lama inside that cap."

"Who did you say?" he asked.

"The Dalai Lama!"

"Who's the Dalai Lama?"

"He's a well-known Buddhist priest—the highest priest in the Buddhist religion."

"Is that right?" Eddie hesitated, as if he was deciding whether to keep the cap on his head.

"What's wrong?"

"Man, you ain't trying to put a hex on me, are you?"

I laughed. "No—if anything the cap will bless you. It may even brighten your smile, even though you hardly ever do smile."

"Man, you sure it ain't gonna do anything to me? 'Cause I never heard of no Dalai Lama."

"No, it ain't! Just let me take your picture, Eddie!"

"Man, OK! Take the picture—but if it comes out stained or

distorted like it's been cursed, then you have to refund me with another one."

"OK, let's do it, Eddie!"

As the Polaroid photograph developed in front of us, a smiling face appeared.

"Man!" he said. "This picture makes me look a lot more human, don't you think so?" He handed me the picture.

"Yeah, it does. But I think you've always been human. You just have to feel it." I gave it back to him.

"Yeah, I'm going to take more pictures like this," he said.

"Well, can I have my cap back now?" I asked.

"Oh, here you go," he said. "Right on! Hey, what's that dude's name again?"

"The Dalai Lama."

"You don't think he made me smile, do you?"

"Why?"

"Well, I don't know," Eddie said, still staring in surprise at the photograph. "It's just that my smile looks a lot more genuine than I felt before you took the picture."

"And how was that?"

"Oh, that I was going to be hexed by wearing your cap!"

We both laughed.

■ ■ ■

San Quentin is really rockin' 'n' rollin' with violence these days. The scheduled execution date of another death row inmate is the chief external reason for it; the internal reason for some, I think, is that we are not finding ways of keeping our release valves open to let out the feelings closing us in.

One guy described it to me by saying, "Last week the ceiling stood five feet above me. Then three days ago it was only one foot, and just last night I got a fucked-up cramp in my neck from trying to sleep on my right side because the goddamn ceiling felt so close to my face that I couldn't switch over to the other side."

We were on the prison yard together. When I suggested that he meditate with me sometime, he just laughed and walked away.

It is so difficult to integrate my meditation practice with all the suffering here. In trying to live a life that reflects the Buddha's ways, I fail continuously! I know so little! I'm just hanging in there with my meditation. Practice is my best companion.

THE EMPOWERMENT CEREMONY

It was noon when my name was called out. A guard handcuffed me and escorted me to the visiting building of the prison. I silently repeated the prayer to Tara as I went, right up to the moment my eyes met Rinpoche's, for the second time in my life.

After ten years of incarceration, I had a real fear of calling myself a Buddhist and of being seen by prisoners in a cross-legged position, praying or meditating. Meditation was for me a quiet practice that, to the extent I could, I kept secret from my fellow prisoners and the prison guards, so it would remain meaningful and pure in my heart when I sat each morning in the most tranquil hour of prison life.

I was especially uneasy about being seen receiving an empowerment, a formal introduction to Vajrayana Buddhism. I'd been denied my request to receive the empowerment in a private prison room. Rinpoche's presence with an interpreter in the visiting room would most likely raise eyebrows. While my heart cherished this opportunity, other voices inside me questioned it. Could this be just a phase I was going through? Would I later betray myself and the sacredness of this empowerment? Was I a Buddhist? Would I take vows that might require me to sacrifice my life? How would I respond to all the violence around me?

In prison, no one believes that conversion to religion is real. Most prisoners think that anyone who suddenly catches religion is playing a game or trying to con their way out of the system. Inmates distance themselves from religious prisoners, believing religion will make them weak.

I had spent almost a year overcoming these doubts, one by

one, through my meditation and Rinpoche's teachings. Yet somehow they had all resurfaced on the morning of the ceremony. The prison echoed with the routine vulgarity of hundreds of inmates cursing, arguing, and yelling all at once. I tried to ignore it, like most mornings when I meditated, but I was too unsettled.

I just sat still, repeating the prayer to Red Tara, the female Buddha, the embodiment of wisdom. Lisa had given this to me long ago to benefit my practice and prepare me for a future empowerment. "Illustrious Tara, please be aware of me, remove my obstacles, and quickly grant my excellent aspirations." With each repetition I searched for the strength to dispel my worries, to open myself fully to the empowerment, to embrace the day of my first proclamation of Buddhism.

I remembered what someone had said to me long ago: "All you need is a pure heart. It's what's in your heart that counts the most. Quietly listen for it." This is what I was doing. I felt fortunate.

I sat down facing Rinpoche through the glass window. With him was Tsering, a close student, who had come to interpret for him. Melody was also there to celebrate this experience with me and, luckily, she took notes. We greeted each other warmly as other prisoners' visitors looked on.

I picked up the phone. Tsering held the phone on their side of the booth. With a bright smile, she asked how I was doing. I smiled back and assured all of them I was doing fine. We were all smiling. Tsering then turned to Rinpoche to receive his words.

She looked back at me. "Rinpoche is asking if your mind is clear."

"Yes, I think so," I replied.

This is my best memory of Rinpoche's words:

"You may feel that your circumstances are hopeless and serve no purpose. But difficulties are not caused by others; they are the result of your own previous thoughts and actions. This is what we call karma—our actions give rise to our future experience.

"Through spiritual practice, we purify the karma we have created in the past while creating the conditions for future happiness and eventual awakening, or enlightenment. We make a commitment: 'I rely on the Buddha; the dharma, the Buddha's teachings; and the sangha, those who practice those teachings. I won't harm anyone with my body, speech, or mind.' If you keep this promise, you won't make future unhappiness for yourself or others. This is called the vow of refuge. It provides for your safety; just like if you don't drink poison, you won't get sick.

"But it's not enough to think only of saving ourselves from suffering, because everyone suffers. People don't realize that only thinking of themselves works against them, resulting in bad karma. That's why we also promise to always think of others, to help them grow in their minds and hearts. But now we aren't fully capable of this, so we do spiritual practice, removing our faults and increasing our capacity to help.

"In your heart, repeat this promise three times: 'I rely on the Buddha, dharma, and sangha. From this day forward, I won't harm anyone. I will work hard on my spiritual practice in order to accomplish the goal of enlightenment, removing all faults and revealing all positive qualities so that I may be of ceaseless benefit to others. That will be my priority every day, even if it costs my life.'"

After a few moments, I repeated this solemn vow.

Rinpoche continued, "Now you have taken the refuge vow and the bodhisattva vow—the vow of one who lives selflessly. Now you are a bodhisattva."

I wanted to make sure I fully understood. "Helping others

could cost me my life in here. Can I qualify my vow by common sense? Can I use my intelligence not to cause my own death?"

"If you help one person today and it costs your life, there is benefit, but only to one person," Rinpoche replied. "But if you train your mind to help in the best way, you'll help many—a hundred, a thousand, countless beings.

"This empowerment is the entrance to Vajrayana Buddhism, a very swift path to enlightenment. Usually the ceremony is done with many ritual objects, but the point is to touch your mind. Because karma is created with our body, speech, and mind, we must purify all three. In Vajrayana Buddhism, we do so by practicing recognizing, through meditation, the inherent purity of our body, speech, and mind. . . .

"One way of understanding the deeper nature of our experience is to think of this life as a dream. Enlightenment is waking up, finding freedom from the dream of suffering. Through meditation we come to realize that everything is like an illusion. . . .

"Just as movies are really only light on cellophane, realize that all this is really the movie of your mind. Try to understand that the true nature of your body, speech, and mind is deathless, faultless, and pure. . . .

"Your thoughts, whether good or bad, just come and go—they're only firings of your brain—whereas the essence of mind is open, present, aware.

"There are two ways to change the mind. One is to think, think, think. The other is to let go of thinking and just let the mind settle. . . .

"From now on, your spiritual practice will involve these three commitments: harmlessness, helpfulness, and purity. Eventually, you will realize your own pure nature. As long as the dream of life seems real, you will feel heaven and hell, experience helpful and harmful people. These are simply the displays of mind's purity and mind's hatred. It's like being surrounded by mirrors—if we are dirty and ugly, that's what we will see. We have to clean ourselves for the image in the mirror to change. It's all a function of mind.

"For example, someone may feel there is nothing worse than living in prison, but a person who lives in a beautiful house might be so miserable that he kills himself. No matter how much you are suffering, there is always someone suffering more. . . .

"Life is impermanent. Whoever is born will die, but we don't know when. All we can be sure of is the present moment. Every moment is a chance to practice these three commitments. This is how we break out of the cycle of karmic existence.

"At the end of every day, confess your negative thoughts and actions and recommit yourself to spiritual practice, taking your vows again. All the merit, the positive energy, that you have created throughout your life, give it to all beings—to victims and aggressors, to animals and all. Every time you do something good, instantly give the merit away."

It sounded so easy when he said it. "I feel pure when I am with you," I told him, "but it's easy to forget."

"Remember the three steps," Rinpoche reminded me. "First, ask for support from Tara. Second, with sincere regret for the harm you have done, confess your mistakes. Third, renew your vows not to harm, to try to help, and to recognize purity. Visualize Tara's blessings in the form of light and nectar washing you, cleansing you, filling you with bliss. Pray and visualize the light and nectar blessing you and all beings."

"If I have wronged someone, do I have to tell them?" I asked.

"It may or may not help. What's most important is to confess within yourself and pray for that other person."

Our visit lasted close to two hours. After the empowerment ended, it became very difficult to hear anything over the phone.

The din of inmates speaking through a chain of phones to their visitors made it a struggle to hear my own. Had the noise been this loud during the empowerment? I felt as if I had taken plugs out of my ears—as though I had just reentered the vast door of prison reality.

At the end of the visit, I thanked Melody for being there and asked her to thank Rinpoche for his many blessings. I told her that I had stopped short of expressing myself fully to him and to Tsering because I had felt so much gratitude welling up and didn't want to be seen in such an emotional state. Melody understood. She hung up the phone and departed, waving goodbye with Rinpoche and Tsering. I waved back.

As I waited for my escort to take me back to my housing unit, an inmate called over to me and asked if I was a practicing Buddhist. I paused. Just as I began to answer, a prison guard came and stood between us to listen in. When I looked at the guard, his eyes wandered away. "Sure I am," I said to the prisoner. I looked at the guard. "There may just be a taste of Buddha in us all."

The guard turned to me with a surprisingly nice smile, and then walked off. I was amazed! I looked back through the window with a powerful sense that Rinpoche was still there. I bowed three times to the empty chair.

. . .

Understanding impermanence, that things are here today and gone tomorrow, really helps. No matter how bad something is, you can remind yourself, "Damn, this won't last long." Then when it doesn't last, you can laugh and say, "I knew it!" What goes around, comes around, and what comes around doesn't last. Everybody gets their turn: the police jump on you, the light goes out, there's a roach in your soup.

My only real hope is to stay in my center, not wishing for something good or fearing something bad. It's very freeing, because if good things happen and you get attached to them, you'll suffer when the bad inevitably comes. You have to learn to accept both.

I know what it feels like to lose a mother. Rinpoche tells a story of a woman whose son dies. She goes to a lama, and he tells her to try to find someone who hasn't lost someone. She goes from house to house, village to village, until she realizes that everyone has lost something or someone. Then she starts to feel more pain for them than for herself. She ends up spending half her time helping others. But that's what heals her.

I imagine that in teaching meditation on the streets, you'd teach people how to better themselves. Here, I learn how not to dive deeper into this hellhole. I've learned more about the things I don't want to do: cuss out other prisoners or guards, argue for two hours about whether or not the lunch meat is spoiled. I don't want to become angry about things like that.

Every effort I make to love means I don't have to feel hatred. When I'm compassionate, all my energy goes in a positive direction, and there's no room for negativity. My tires can't go backward, they can only roll forward.

ANGRY FACES

"Man, Jarvis. Are you watching the news?" my new neighbor asked from the next cell one evening. I was relaxing, reading a book about meditation.

"I have it on, Omar, but I'm not really watching it," I answered, glancing up at my television. "Why, what's up?"

"Ah, man! Check out Channel Seven. They showing a Ku Klux Klan rally in Louisiana. Man, just look at all those Klansmen screaming and shouting all that white supremacy garbage. Get this: all these idiots is talking about how all the Jews and Blacks is destroying this country. Did you hear what they were saying?"

"Nah, man. I missed it. I have the volume turned down. I'm just using the light to read by. I did see a bunch of angry faces and racist posters, though."

"Oh, OK," said Omar. "Man, I apologize. I didn't mean to take you away from your reading."

"Hey, that's OK. I don't min' you calling over to me about something big in the news. If you see something interesting, let me know."

"Right, right on! I can do that," said Omar, ending our conversation.

About ten minutes later, Omar hollered, "Hey, Jarvis!

Man, check out all those people. It must be a thousand folks marching in San Francisco. Do you see them?"

"Wow!" I said, looking up at the huge demonstration on my screen. "What's up with them?"

"Man, it's an environmentalist demonstration. They demanding an end to the cutting of trees in some places, and all the senseless slaughter of wildlife animals. They saying the planet is being destroyed and more and more kinds of animals is near extinction."

"Is that right? I can tell just by looking that they're upset. You see that one woman raging into the microphone and those demonstrators holding up posters and shouting and getting arrested? Hey, they all must be pretty pissed to be screaming like that and risking going to jail."

A little later Omar yelled, "Hey, check that out. Are you still watching? Look at the president and all those congressmen, right there on national TV, fighting and arguing, each trying to convince the public that the other is at fault for this terrible economy."

"Yeah, I see them. Is that what they're fussing about? I can tell they're in an uproar about something. That one senator, man, he's almost spitting. But you know what's really interesting, Omar?"

"No, what's that?"

"Well, for the first time, I'm starting to see something—that the anger and bitterness on the faces of these congressmen and the president of the United States is the same as on the faces of all those environmentalists and the Klansmen. The only difference is that the Klansmen wore khaki and hoods, the demonstrators were dressed for going to jail, while the congressmen and the president wore real expensive suits."

"I never seen it like that," said Omar. "I get mad when I see the Klan on TV or when I see all what's goin' down. But I never thought until now, Jarvis, that we all wear the same hateful expression."

"Yeah, isn't it a trip?" I said. "But it's something to think about—learning to see everyone's suffering, not just the frustration of those we agree with. Otherwise, let's be honest, all we really want to do is kick a few Klansmen's asses."

"Ah, man . . . man . . . man!" Omar groaned. "I don't think I'll be able to do that. That there is a little too much chile on my hot dog for me."

MAXISM

When one of my friends sent me an excellent poem she had written about AIDS, I knew I needed to share it with my friend Max, who has AIDS. Because he was housed on a different tier in the unit, the only way I could show it to him was to smuggle it out onto the exercise yard. Prison rules strictly forbid anything to be taken outside.

As Max and I were walking around in the freezing cold, I talked to him about using his experience with the disease to teach other young people about drugs and safe sex. After about an hour, it began to rain. There aren't any shelters in the yard, so Max and I kept walking along the fence. I hoped the rain would stop so that I could show him the poem, but it didn't. Even so, it seemed a perfect time to share the poem, so I stopped Max and handed it to him.

He seemed surprised that this Buddhist still knew how to smuggle things out of the unit. He smiled as he unfolded it, reading the poem aloud, as raindrops fell on the paper. I tried to shield it with my hands, but it was raining way too hard. By the time he was halfway through, much of the black ink had washed away. It was as if the rain was melting the words into our souls.

My own immediate reaction was "Impermanence!" For the whole hour I had been trying to explain impermanence to Max and here it was! The words had been there and then they were completely gone.

Sometime later, Max said to me, "Man, that whole trip we had—with that cool poem from your friend—even though it could almost make a grown man weep, it gave me the weirdest feeling that when I die, I'll be back."

"What do you mean?" I asked.

"Hey, man," said Max as the rain poured down on us, "I got the feeling that when I die things is going to happen and I'll be back on the scene again—probably as a mouse or rabbit or something—but that this isn't the end, you know?"

"Man," I said to him, "that sounds to me like a bit of Buddhism."

"Maybe so," said Max, "but, shit, for right now, I'm just going to call it Maxism."

JOE BOB

I had almost fallen asleep when Louis Farrakan came on some-one's radio, blasting all over the tier.

"Hey, can I get a little respect?" my neighbor hollered.

"Who in the fuck are you?"

"Say, man, I'm Joe Bob down here in cell ninety-four, ask-ing that you give me and the people on this fuckin' tier a little respect."

"Say, Joe Bob, or whatever your name is, this is Khali in cell seventy-three, and if you want me to turn down my radio that's too damn bad. This is prison, and if you can't stand the noise then you shouldn't have brought your damn ass here."

"You know what?" said Joe Bob. "All I'm asking for is a little respect. It's almost one o'clock in the morning, and what you are doing is very disrespectful."

"Man, check this out! This is San Quentin. I do what the fuck I wanna do. I wouldn't care if it was three o'clock."

"You think so, huh?" said Joe Bob. "We'll see if you have the same attitude tomorrow when these cells come open. We'll see what you're made out of then."

"Are you threatening me?" said Khali.

"Do you feel threaten'?"

"Yeah, it sounds like a threat, punk!"

"OK, then," said Joe Bob, "that's just what it is. Consider yourself threaten'."

"Man, you go fuck yourself," Khali hollered, turning his radio up full blast.

"Say, Joe Bob," I said. "You shouldn't even trip off that dumb shit down the way. You been in this joint for almost fifteen years."

"No, fuck that. I tried talking to that guy with some kind of respect. I asked him nicely. But he wants to be big and tough about it. I'll kill that fucker."

"It ain't worth it, Joe Bob," I said. "Just let it go. Let it go."

"Jay, man, I'm a convict, you dig? I been in these prisons all my life. I treat everyone with respect. I'll give my last to another con. He can have the shirt off my back, you dig? I don't care what color he is . . . black, white, blue, or green—a con is a con. I don't disrespect no one in no shape, form, or fashion!"

"Yeah, I know what you're sayin', Joe Bob, but—"

"Nah, man," he said. "That dude down there, he ain't no convict, the way he plays games and disrespects the rest of us on the tier. I be honest with you, Jarvis. I take offense at inmates, dudes like him that don't get it, especially those who tries to start racial problems."

"Yeah, I know what you're sayin' but—"

"Jarvis, I don't care if that dude listens to his black leader's speeches, but when he tries to make me listen, then he's making me do his time, his program, and I do my own program."

"Yeah, I hear you. I know exactly where you're coming from."

"I'm just an old country white boy," he said. "I get along with everyone. I don't play no racial games. I respect all races."

"Yeah, I know, Joe Bob, but just listen to me for a second," I pleaded. "This prison ain't what it use' to be. There's not just convicts here anymore. The people coming to the joint now are younger, more immature, and don't have the common courtesy most of us have for the next man. And that guy down the way playing that shit, he thinks it's a game, Joe Bob."

"Yeah, right," said Joe Bob. "You better tell him something, then, before I end his life, his whole fuckin' world."

"Don't worry, Joe Bob, I'll speak with him tomorrow. Just give me that opportunity, OK?"

"Yeah, you got that coming," he said. "Maybe you can talk some sense to him. He'll probably listen to you since you're black."

"Yeah, I think he will. He thinks I and other blacks is listening to Farrakan. He just don't know the trouble he is creating on this tier, stirring racial tensions."

After a while Joe Bob said, "Say, Jarvis, you know if it was a white dude playing his radio, I'd be telling him the same thing. Believe me, it ain't a white-black thing. I don't care who it is. It's a respect thing, you dig?"

"Yeah, I know this, Joe Bob."

"OK, Jarvis. I think I'll turn in. I'll check with you tomorrow."

"Right, I'll see you in the morning. But one more thing, Joe Bob," I said.

"What's that?"

"I don't want to hear you over there fuckin' with your wall-safe, pullin' out no weapon, you understand? Just let me handle this, OK?"

"Hey, Jarvis, that's on my word! You ain't going to hear me digging in my wall for anything. What I'm doing now," he said, "is putting it back. I was ready to kill that boy come first light."

"That's why I had to talk to you before the lights come on. You don't need no more murders."

***

Every night before I go to sleep, I lay my thin mattress on the floor. I've been sleeping there for more than ten years because I enjoy the king-size bed of the floor, plus I use the bunk portion of my cell as my office space. I keep all my books, radio, TV, and everything else on the steel slab, and just sleep on the floor, because I am usually at the office fourteen to sixteen hours a day, and I sleep only a few hours.

When I woke up a while ago, there were ants crawling all over me. I just watched them for a few minutes, until it became obvious I had to do something. I got up, placed a few sugar cubes in a cup of water, and made a trail for the ants to follow out of my cell. So far, it's working pretty well. Tomorrow, though, when the guards see them, they'll spray and kill the poor creatures. But I've done too much practice these past days to destroy that well-earned karma by killing ants. No way!

TYLENOL PRAYER BEADS

It was past midnight. The prison night watchman was making his routine body count down the tier when I awakened from a late evening snooze with plans to get up and spend the rest of the night doing my meditation practice.

I paced the length of my cell for a while, all eight feet of it, preparing myself with repetitions of the Tara prayer. Suddenly I was struck by an idea for a way to make my own mala, my own prayer beads, which I could use to keep track of the repetitions. I spun around my cell, looking for what I would need.

Since the very first day of learning this prayer, I'd wanted a mala to help me with my practice. My teacher, Rinpoche, and other practitioners who came to San Quentin to visit me had often offered to bring me one, but prison authorities had denied them permission to do so.

I gathered a pair of prison-issue jeans, a *Sports Illustrated*, and a bottle of Tylenol, and sat down at the front of my cell. I picked and pulled at the seams of the jeans until I got hold of a good piece of thread. I unraveled more than I meant to. "Uh-oh!" A gaping hole widened down the leg. "I'll get another pair somehow," I resolved, and put the thread aside.

I opened the *Sports Illustrated* to the middle and took out one of the staples. I straightened it out and sharpened it on the rough concrete floor beside me. I had to be very quiet. If the night watchman heard these strange scratching sounds, the whole cell block might be searched in a panic. Scraping usually meant a weapon was being sharpened.

For almost an hour I ground the staple on the floor, until it was as sharp as a sewing needle.

Now I opened the bottle of Tylenol and began the slow process of poking a tiny hole in the center of each tablet. There were a hundred of them. I had to be as careful as a surgeon. First I poked at the surface of the Tylenol and then with a screwing motion I made a hole all the way through. Taking the thread from my jeans, I passed it through each "bead."

All through the night I sat cross-legged, poking holes in Tylenols and threading them together. It was extremely tedious. My eyes blurred with exhaustion. My fingers began to get sore. I felt foolish. "What in the world am I doing?" I asked myself. But I kept going, determined to finish.

Five and a half hours later I held my first mala, made from trouser thread and Tylenols. I was elated. But when I got up to stretch, my head throbbed—I had an awful headache. I stood silently at the bars of my cell, taking comfort in looking out a window in the opposite wall. A beautiful morning light was peeking in. "I wouldn't mind a Tylenol or two," I thought, "to stop this pounding in my head." I looked down at my hands. "Damn! I don't have any. They're all on this mala."

For a split second I thought the unthinkable, my head was hurting that much. Then I smiled. I realized that after spending all this time making my Tylenol mala, all I needed to do was to sit my butt back down with it and take a few moments—no Tylenols—to do my spiritual practice.

■ ■ ■

Meditation has become something I cannot do without. I see and hear more clearly, feel more relaxed and calm, and I actually find my experiences slowing down. I'm more appreciative of each day as I observe how things constantly change and dissolve. I've realized that everything is in a continual process of coming and going. I don't hold happiness or anger for a long time. It just comes and goes.

I'm beginning to learn how to meditate during other daily activities. This evening I tried to meditate while a Chicago Bulls vs. Detroit Pistons basketball game was on TV. I couldn't avoid hearing the game and the prisoners' cheering. It was extremely loud. Even worse, I like basketball.

I didn't last a full quarter of the game. I had my eyes closed, trying not to listen. But I couldn't do it. I kept trying and trying—just sitting there on my floor. But when by accident I let out a cheer—having heard that Michael Jordan hit a three-pointer—I got up and said, "OK, OK. Maybe next time." I just didn't have the concentration. At least not yet.

I'm not a great meditator, but I realize how important my practice is. Still, I also like watching sports, playing basketball, and looking at cartoons. I adore junk foods and sometimes I love dirty jokes. I'm in love with life.

PEACE ACTIVIST

When I awoke in the early morning to begin my meditation practice, I tried to envision myself as a peace activist in the rough neighborhood of my prison tier. The night before, the once-empty cell adjacent to mine had been filled with the raging of a new inmate. Although his loud voice had filtered into my deep sleep, I refused, as I did every night, to awaken, to lose that very comfortable place that finally made sleeping on a hard concrete prison floor easy.

Now, in the light of dawn appearing in the window opposite my cell, I quietly placed my folded blanket on the cold floor. My new neighbor began to scream again. "I kill you . . . I kill you all, you damn sons a bitches, if y'all don't let me out of here!"

I could see in my mind his hands shaking and rattling his cell bars. I wondered if I could be just as determined to sit in meditation as I had been to sleep through this thunder of human rage reverberating throughout the housing unit. My teacher, Rinpoche, had once sent me a transcript of one of his teachings, where he mentioned a kind of joy that he felt while meditating at airports, waiting for the flights on his busy schedule.

I wished I could remember *why* he liked this! I decided the answer could be found in something else Rinpoche had said: that there was no time to lose in practicing meditation. I was eager to try this kind of meditation. I could usually meditate within ear range of lots of noise, but nothing as loud and close as my neighbor's steel bars vibrating like a jumbo jet breaking through the skies.

I was only minutes into my practice when my neighbor called over to me. "Hey, dude in the next cell. Save me half of that damn cigarette."

Huh? I thought, my mantra interrupted. I hadn't smoked in years. I imagined someone asking Rinpoche a question like that while he was sitting at the airport. No, they wouldn't dare! I chuckled silently.

I could smell someone smoking in one of the cells not far from mine. I had become accustomed to the smoking habits of my fellow prisoners. On my best days I simply accepted the morning scent as my prison brand of incense. With each lit cigarette, the atmosphere became a smoky shrine for my meditation.

When the wall between me and my neighbor started to move as if an earthquake had hit, I was half tempted to ask him to knock off the banging and join me in meditation. But he would have taken it as an insult, which would only have made me a target for his rage, and his mission in life to make our adjacent living situation pure misery for us both. So I tried to quiet my mind, still sitting on my blanket, still wanting to meditate.

"Hey, dude in the next cell," my neighbor shouted again, pounding on the wall. "Let me have a few tokes of that cigarette. Man, I know you smokin' over there. I know you hear me, man!" He kept shouting and banging.

"Hey, hey!" I yelled. I'd finally had enough and by now was totally convinced I was no Rinpoche. "Man! You don't need to shout and go on beating the wall like a damn fool!" I stepped up to my cell bars. "Man, whatever your name is, that is not me smoking. I don't smoke. I haven't smoked in years. And even if I did smoke, check: the way you've been shouting and beating on that poor wall all morning—which, mind you, has been tryin' to mind its own business, just like me, man—I wouldn't give you jack shit, OK?"

"Ah, man." My neighbor tried to calm his voice. "They call me Bosshog. And all I want is a damn smoke, you know?"

"Well, I'm Jarvis," I replied, "and all I want is my freedom. Believe me, Bosshog, this is not to say that I want it more than you want a cigarette right about now, because I know what cigarettes can make you feel. But by beating on the wall, you're taking what little freedom I have away from me, and that ain't cool, you know?"

"OK, but do you think you can find me a cigarette?" my neighbor pleaded. "I swear to God, man, I've been needing a cigarette all morning, like poor folk in hell need ice water!"

I laughed. I liked the way Bosshog put it—that only poor people needed ice water in hell. As for a cigarette, I always kept extra things for inmates like Bosshog. I would collect old magazines and novels and purchase inexpensive soap and toothpaste and cheap smoking tobacco. I had vowed to do this fifteen years back, when I arrived at San Quentin and had to use kitchen butter from my breakfast tray on my badly chapped skin because I had no money to buy lotion from the prison commissary.

"Yeah, I think I can find you a bit of tobacco and some rolling papers," I told him. I sensed from my many years of having neighbors of all sorts that he was one of so many youngsters flooding the prison system for smoking crack or violating their parole.

"But you have to stay cool and not go disturbing the peace on the tier again," I added. "Will you give me your word?"

There was a long silence. To me, this meant Bosshog was taking his word seriously. This made him a rare bird: few new prisoners took even a second before saying anything for a free cigarette.

"Yeah, man," he finally answered. "You drive a hard bargain, but you got a deal! I'll keep it all on cool, my word, man."

"OK, give me a minute." I walked to the back of my cell and rummaged in the box underneath my bunk. I found more than half of a six-ounce can of tobacco left. I had no intention of giving it all to Boss. It was likely that other newcomers would need some, too. Also, the length of time it had taken Boss to decide to accept our agreement probably meant that it would be a struggle for him to keep his end of the bargain. By rationing the tobacco I would keep him at bay.

I looked around my cell for something to wrap the tobacco in. I had a photocopy of Thich Nhat Hanh's book *Being Peace* that a friend had mailed me. Later, a paperback copy of the book itself had been sent to me from a bookstore, so I reckoned it wouldn't hurt to wrap the tobacco in one of the photocopy pages. And besides, I thought, Thich Nhat Hanh might appeal to the Bosshog, one page at a time.

"Hey, Boss, do you have a fishline over there?"

"I found one under the bunk," he answered. "Your last neighbor must have left it."

He quickly threw the fishline in front of my cell. I retrieved it, using my own, then tied on the tobacco rolled in paper and watched Boss pull it in.

"Man, right on! Righteous!" he exclaimed happily. "I really appreciate all this smoke!"

"No problem. Perhaps I can send you more in a day or so, you know?"

"Oh, this is cool, real cool!" said Bosshog.

The bright sun shining through the window told me there wasn't much of the morning left to sit in meditation, but it also ushered in a quiet feeling of having done something as a simple kind of peace activist. Boss had stayed quiet, and the other prisoners hadn't said a word against him moving into our neighborhood.

Over the next months, I kept on sending Boss a daily supply of tobacco, always wrapped in a page of *Being Peace*. Boss was still a bit off his rocker, but I began to consider him a kind of brother. One page at a time he came to like Thich Nhat Hanh. Every now and then, Boss even tried his best to meditate, but he was never able to stay awake early in the morning, as he put it, "to go on some ol' meditation trip with you, Jay."

After eighteen months Bosshog was released from the grip of San Quentin and from dependence on me for tobacco and *Being Peace*. Before he walked off the tier, he stood in front of my cell and together we recited what had become Boss's mantra—something he'd learned to say whenever he was about to blow his top. We always started off chanting in unison with the words "Man, man," and then, "If we are peaceful, if we are happy, we can smile, and everyone in our family, our entire society will benefit from our peace."

. . .

I was walking out on the exercise yard last week, along the fence, star-ing up at the beautiful clear sky. It was a gorgeous day. Then some-thing frightening happened: someone got stabbed on the adjacent yard. In the gunmen's tower, prison guards were racking rounds into their rifles. They were shouting at two guys scuffling and fighting and trying to kill each other. I knew immediately that someone was going to die. Either the guards or one of these two prisoners would be respon-sible for taking a human being's life.

The tower gunmen ordered everyone to lie facedown on the ground as they swung their fully loaded rifles around the three adjacent yards. I didn't know what to think. Since I didn't hear any gunshots, I fig-ured the two guys must have stopped fighting. At least the gunmen had been saved from taking someone's life. But what about the prisoner who had been stabbed? Was he dead? What had I been thinking about before all this happened? Why am I lying here like this? Is this all real? Shit! How long can I go on trying to be a Buddhist in this prison cul-ture that has me lying facedown? Who am I kidding?

Just as I thought my head would explode from so many flashing thoughts, I locked on to a single idea: how some people in this world have only a tragic five seconds to put their entire lives in order before they die—in a car crash or in some other sudden way. I realized that what really matters isn't where we are or what's going on around us, but what's in our hearts while it's happening.

I used to feel I could hide inside my practice, that I could simply sit and contemplate the raging anger of a place like this, seeking inner peace through prayers of compassion. But now I believe love and com-passion are things to extend to others. It's a dangerous adventure to share them in a place like S.Q. Yet I see now that we become better people if we can touch a hardened soul, bring joy into someone's life, or just be an example for others, instead of hiding behind our silence.

The key is in using what we know. This calls for lots of practice. There is this vast space in life to do just that, both as a practitioner and as someone who walks around the same prison yard as everyone else in this place. I've learned how to accept responsibility for the harm I've caused others by never letting myself forget the things I did and by using those experiences to help others understand where they lead.

FOURTH OF JULY

The fourth of July had almost gone unnoticed when I heard someone down the tier arguing with a prison guard.

"Hey, all I'm asking you for is a fuckin' spoon to eat with when you serve the evening chow tonight."

"No can do!" Two unfamiliar guards with no name tags on their uniforms had begun their evening shift with a body count of all of us locked in our single-man cells.

"So you guys wanna be assholes, eh? Well, OK. I can be an asshole too!" I recognized Bernard's voice.

"Man, what's up, Bernard?" my neighbor Billy asked after the guards left the tier.

"Hey, man, they have these two new goons with an attitude working our tier tonight," said Bernard. "They don't want to give me a spoon to eat with, you know?"

"Yeah, I know," said Billy. "I just asked them for some toilet paper and they straight out shined me on, too."

"Hey, Jarvis," Bernard hollered. "Did you catch that? What's up with those guards?"

"I don't really know," I said, "but they've never worked on this tier before, so they probably don't know about issuing spoons and things when we need them. I wouldn't sweat it too much. They'll get the hang of it."

"Yeah, I hope you're right, Jarvis," said Bernard, "because, man, I don't see any animals on this damn tier—not unless they want to turn me into one, you know?"

"Chill out, Bernard," I said. "They'll give you a spoon, man—they have to."

"Well, they better bring me some toilet paper, too!" said Billy. "Man, I'd much rather eat with my hands than have to wipe my fat white ass with them." Everyone laughed.

An hour later the meal cart came speeding down the tier. The two new guards began serving evening chow at the end cell when all hell broke loose.

"Man, don't be throwing the food in my damn tray like that," someone hollered at the guards when they got to his cell.

"Man, what the hell are you doing? I'm no fuckin' animal!" someone else shouted.

"You fuckin' dog-ass pig, what's wrong with you?" another prisoner yelled. Everyone in the back cells began shouting and screaming.

"All you fuckin' cry babies, shut up," one of the guards shouted and hurried down the tier, pushing the chow cart from cell to cell.

"You fuckin' goons came to work with your bitch-ass attitudes and now you wanna take it out on us, eh?" said Maddog, when the guards got to his cell. "What happen', your ugly-ass wife didn't give you none last night?"

"No, I'm getting it from your wife, didn't she tell you?" said one of the guards.

"I use your wife to bone every night; the whore is good, too!" said the other guard, laughing.

"You fuckin' pig! Just open my cell door," Maddog yelled with rage. "Come on, come on." He rattled his cell bars violently. "Just open my cell door and we'll see who you'll be fuckin' tonight, man. I'll kill your asses."

"Oh, is that right?" said the guard, placing Maddog's food on his tray port.

"Yeah, you fuckin' right!" shouted Maddog hurling his tray off the port. "You ain't goin' to feed me like I'm some damn animal, sloppin' my food all over the place."

"Well, starve then," the guard said, moving the chow cart toward Bernard's cell.

"All I need is a spoon," said Bernard.

"No can do!" replied the guard. "You can ask your regular tier officer for a spoon tomorrow."

"So what in the hell do I eat with?"

"Your hands, I suppose, I don't know."

"Man, go fuck yourself, pig!" screamed Bernard through his cell bars. "Get that cart out of here before I throw some piss in your goddamn face, punk!"

"I love you too," the guard smiled, blowing him a mock kiss.

"Yeah, keep playin' with me," Bernard yelled, as the guard moved to the next cell. "I'll have somethin' waiting for your ass when you back on the tier. Punk, you best learn who you fuckin' wit'!"

"Man, what about that damn toilet paper I asked you for?" Billy called to the guards. He paid no attention to the chow cart as it was wheeled in front of his cell.

"You'll just have to use something else tonight," said the guard. "Because I'm not here to do anything but feed and that's it. This is overtime for me, and I've been here sixteen long hours. I have a Fourth of July party waiting for me when I leave Quentin tonight. So you inmates can expect nothing until your regular tier cop comes on tomorrow."

"Man!" shouted Billy. "Hey, just because you're working overtime don't mean you don't 'posed to do your job. You can't deprive me of basic necessities."

The guards pushed the chow cart away from his cell.

"Hey, man, where are you goin'? I didn't get my fuckin' tray, man!"

"You've been fed already," said one of the guards, now in front of my cell.

"Man, no, I didn't get any chow."

"Yes, you have your food tray," the guard insisted.

"Whoa! Wait a minute," I interrupted angrily. "Sir, you never fed my neighbor. He was asking for something else and you just forgot to feed him."

"No, we didn't forget," the guards smirked.

"Oh, I see! You just don't want to feed him, eh? The same way you don't want to bring him any toilet paper, or don't want to give the other prisoner down the tier a spoon. You shining people on and feeding everybody like animals. Just because you're tired and don't work on this tier don't mean you don't 'posed to conduct yourself like professionals. You assholes are taking a chance of getting hurt by someone on this damn tier."

My anger was getting the best of me.

"This is our job," one of the guards mocked. "Now what about you, do you want to eat?" he asked.

"No, get the hell away from me, too." My gut tightened. I realized I had probably said too much.

After the guards had gone, I could hear the voices of men much angrier than I vowing to retaliate when the guards returned in several hours for a routine tier count.

The cold, deadly stillness that descended on the tier gave away what some of my fellow prisoners were planning. I lay down, trying to convince myself that whatever happened to these two jerks was no business of mine.

"These cops are complete idiots!" I reflected angrily. Why had they stirred things up so much that my fellow prisoners were preparing to take their heads? They would come back on the tier, and without the slightest hesitation someone would stab them.

"But who'll do it?" I wondered. "They all want to!"

Slowly, an awareness grew inside me. The guards had been

idiots, but nothing they had said or done would ever justify their murder. I jumped off my bunk to get a drink of water at the sink. I needed to figure something out in the next hour, before those goons came back on the tier. But what?

I slowly poured what was left from my cup back into the sink. Then it hit me. Why not flood the tier? Why not get everyone to channel their murderous rage into flooding the whole damn tier?

The idea made perfect sense to me, but would my fellow prisoners go for it? I didn't waste any time finding out.

"Hey, Billy, what are you doing over there?" I called to my neighbor, knocking on the wall between us and breaking the silence on the tier.

"Man, you know what I'm doin'," he said. "I'm waitin' just like everyone else. I got my shit ready for those two punks!"

"Yeah, man," I said. "I can feel the vibes. But I was thinking. These cops didn't just treat *you* like some animal; they were assholes to all of us, you know? So whatever we do, we should do it together. You hear me?"

"I hear what you're sayin'," said Billy. "Bud, that sounds right!"

"Hey, what about you, Bernard?" I asked.

"Yeah, I hear you," said Bernard.

"What about Maddog—man, can you hear me down there?" I spoke louder, hoping to be heard by the whole tier, but not by the guards.

"Yeah, I can hear you now," said Maddog. "But I really didn't catch it all."

"I know that everyone got something weighing on them," I said, "but we're turning a minor incident into something deadly serious, you know? How many people in San Quentin today burglarized someone's house, but messed up somehow and ended up in this penitentiary for murder? It would be really stupid to catch assault or murder charges on a guard over a thing like this!"

"Man, I don't mind killing one of those goons," someone said. "That one pig pushing the food cart tonight who purposely stuck his nasty-ass fingers in my food, he needs to die."

"No, man!" I said. "You don't mean that! Death is too permanent. What you mean is that he should feel the way you do. And you're not dead, right? So check it out."

I felt I had the attention of all seventeen prisoners on the tier.

"These guards want to treat us like animals, so they can make easy overtime money and then go home to their Fourth of July party. Well, let's just flood the tier and keep them here all night."

"Yeah, that's not a bad idea," Billy said. "Man, the water'll be up to their knees. All we have to do is stuff towels down our toilets and keep flushing them until the water overflows. Hey, what do you think, Maddog?"

"Honestly, I want to down one of those fools," Maddog answered. "But Jay did make a good point. So whatever you all want to do, I'm for it just as long as these pigs get a dose of their own medicine."

"Man, that'll be so funny." Bernard began laughing. "Those pigs think that all they gonna do is straight kick back and wait until their shift's over. Can you imagine what it'll be like when they come back on the tier and see that they have to walk through four feet of toilet water and, on top of that, can't go home to their Fourth of July party until it's all cleaned up? Man, they are going to straight-out flip!"

"Man, are you sure they'll have to stay to clean it up?" someone asked.

"Hell, yeah!" Bernard answered. "Flooding is a safety and security hazard. In fact, a lot of guards from other cell blocks will be forced to come and help, too."

"So what are we waiting for?" I said before they could change their minds and contemplate something more drastic again. "Let's do it!"

"Man, I already got started," said Maddog. "I got everything off my floor and my towel stuffed down my toilet."

"Whoa, wait a minute," someone called out. They all needed some time to get their own things off the floor. I wasn't surprised by their cheerfulness as they readied themselves. I, too, quickly picked up my mattress and belongings and set them on my bunk.

Then we began pushing the buttons of our toilets. With each flush, the water flowed over the edges of the toilet bowls, until a great rushing sound came roaring over the tier.

"Man, keep flushing, keep flushing!" someone yelled.

"Man! This is fuckin' great!" said Billy.

"Hey, man, I really pray to God those two pigs think so too!" said Bernard as everyone cheered, their joy flooding the tier.

Knives and zip guns had been replaced by something as simple as water.

Then, mysteriously, all the toilets shut off.

"What the hell happened?" asked Billy.

"Those pigs must've hit the main switch," said Bernard, "because everything is off—the toilets and the sinks!"

"Well, there goes our Fourth of July party, eh?" someone joked. "Shit man, what do y'all think—are the coppers going to raid the joint, take us all downtown to jail for questioning, or what?"

"Yeah, right!" said Bernard. "Right to San fuckin' Quentin!" The whole tier burst out laughing.

The loud joking didn't subside when the guards returned to the tier, slowly walking from cell to cell with anger written all over their faces.

"Man, check out their plastic boots," someone said. "These cops are trying to wear eight-inch boots in four feet of water!"

"Hey, officer, officer," someone else yelled. "What a helluva Fourth of July party, eh? I'm so glad you can stay and be a part of it all. Man, isn't it a splash?"

"No, it isn't!" one of the guards shot back, continuing slowly down the tier.

"Hey, man, what about my damn toilet paper?" asked Billy.

"You get your toilet paper when we're finished."

"So when will that be?"

"Whenever we get this goddamn water cleaned up," said the guard. The tier erupted into laughter once again. "You fuckin' people are going to have our asses here way into the wee hours of the night! You'll get your toilet paper when we're done."

"What about the sinks and toilets? When will they be turned back on?" I asked.

"After you are thrown in solitary confinement!" the guard answered. "Mister, you are going to the Hole!"

"Who me? Why am I going to the Hole?" I asked.

"For inciting inmates to flood, that's why!" one of the guards retorted angrily.

"You sure it was me? Man, why would I do something like that?" I asked.

"Oh, we know it was you! And while you're in the Hole, you'll have a very, very long time to ask yourself why."

I smiled at the guards standing at my cell. Being thrown in the Hole was worth the pleasure of seeing them still alive.

STOP! A BUDDHIST IS HERE!

We had been out on the exercise yard for an hour when I noticed a new prisoner approaching the yard gate, looking like a woman. I couldn't believe it. No San Quentin exercise yard hated homosexuals more than this one. Gays came in second only to informants as candidates for stabbings and killings. I knew this was some kind of mistake, or a dirty ploy by the prison administration to get someone killed. Wondering which of these two evils it could be, I glanced up at the tower gunmen.

I'd personally never held anything against homosexuals, but I knew how many of these prisoners felt about them. Some hated them just for hate's sake. Fear motivated others—especially those who had arrived at San Quentin in the early eighties with life sentences or were on death row and had long ago been taken in by the first media reports that AIDS was exclusively a homosexual disease. Later, prison officials told us that other diseases like tuberculosis were being spread throughout the prisons by homosexuals. The men on the yard had come to believe all this.

"This guy isn't going to last one full hour out here!" I thought. I didn't have to turn around to know that there were other prisoners behind me, looking on coldly, pulling prison-made shanks out of their waistbands. I could feel it. There was silence everywhere. I wanted so badly to holler out and warn this stupid person, "Man, this isn't your damn yard. Don't bring your ass out here." But I couldn't do this. I couldn't say anything. It would have been considered snitching. So I swallowed, kept my mouth shut, and prayed.

Then came a loud clinking and whining as the motorized gate was lifted to let this person onto the yard. When the gate slammed shut, my heart dropped. He had just become a walking dead man. I had seen a few others like this throughout my many years of incarceration.

Everyone in the yard, from those on the basketball and handball courts, to the scattered groups over by the pullup bar, watched in silence as this fragile man with tiny breasts, his hair in a ponytail, Vaseline on his lips, dressed in tight state jeans, began swishing along the yard fence.

I looked up again at the gunmen hovering over the exercise yard and saw that they had already gotten in position. They both had their semiautomatic rifles hanging over the gun rail, readying themselves to fire down on the north wall. Obviously, they knew what everybody else did.

According to the laws of prison life, none of this was supposed to be any business of mine. But it was. This time it had to be. For all the life in me, I couldn't look at this gay person, sitting alone against the back wall of the exercise yard, and not see an innocent human being. Yet I could not summon up the courage to become a snitch and risk my own life to warn him off this yard. Why me, anyway? I felt crossed up.

I had to do something. I began walking along the wall. Dammit. Why were things like this happening more often since I had taken my vows? What would all those people outside these walls who call themselves Buddhists tell me to do? Would they say, "Let's all be Buddhists and just put our knives away and smile?"

I made my way around to where the gay man was sitting. I passed him several times without stopping, so I could get a good look at him. I wanted to find out if he was aware of what was going on, aware that someone was about to stab him. The fool was not! He sat there like a tiny fish in a shark tank. I needed to think fast, because time was running out. I had to get away from this guy, quick.

I spotted Crazy Dan on the opposite side of the exercise yard. He was squatting, surreptitiously cuffing a long shank in the sleeve of his coat. "Damn!" I muttered. My head began to pound as I watched Dan, a good friend of mine, prepare to knife this innocent person. I had known Dan for more than eight years in San Quentin, and I didn't want him to end his own life trying to take someone else's with two ready gunmen watching.

Then my mind went blank. I began walking along the wall, on the opposite side of the yard from Dan. It wasn't until we both turned the corners and faced each other, with the lone gay man sitting quietly against the back wall, that I saw the shank slowly slide down Dan's coat sleeve into his right hand. I quickened my pace to get to the man before he did. I didn't have time to be scared, or even to think. I just knew I had to get there first.

Quickly, I knelt in front of the gay man and asked if he had a spare cigarette. Dan was only six feet away. I looked up and saw him stopped dead, with his right hand hiding behind his leg, gripping the long shank. He was stunned. I could sense the adrenaline coursing through his body. His eyes, like those of a ferocious beast, stared into mine. I'd never seen those eyes before—they were not the eyes of the Dan I knew. For that split second I thought my friend was going to kill me.

Then something happened. Dan blinked hard several times. He must have realized my silent plea. Maybe he remembered the time I'd stood by him when he too had been marked for death. He turned, and calmly walked away.

"Hey, Daddy, did you want this cigarette or what?" the man asked in a female voice, holding one out to me.

"No, I don't smoke."

He looked around, confused.

When I realized what I had just done, I almost choked on my fear. Why had I put my life on the line for somebody I didn't know or hadn't even seen before? "Am I crazy or just plain stupid?" I wondered, looking in the face of this person who was still totally unaware of what had just happened.

I stood up and walked away, knowing that I would take a lot of heat later that day out on the exercise yard. But I figured I could make the case—which I truly believed—that all this had been one big setup, that the prison authorities had been intent on shooting and killing some of us, and that I wasn't about to let anybody that I knew, especially Crazy Dan, get killed by walking into their trap. The truth, which I would leave out, was that I did it for the gay man, too. He meant nothing to me—except that he was as human as the rest of us. He never came back to our yard after that day, but the incident left me with many questions.

Am I alone? Am I the only Buddhist out here? Does this mean that I, the Lone Buddhist Ranger, am expected to try to stop this madness by myself? I imagined myself raising my hand and yelling, "Stop! A Buddhist is here!"

I can't stop it. It isn't stopping. There are stabbings every day in this place. All I have is my spiritual practice. Every morning and night I fold my blanket under me and meditate on the floor of my cell.

ON THE QUESTION OF TIME

When we think of what seems like the enormous amount of time we have in life, we all have a tendency to put things off that we could do today. This is because we live with promises that life is long and that time is constantly on our side.

This is despite the fact that every day, in the news or closer to home, we are shown how suddenly our lives can become shorter or swept away. All throughout our life experiences, we're impacted in some way. But the scenes of car accidents, plane and train crashes, and so many, many more tragic events show us how time, as the precious essence for our being on earth, is always worth taking, every moment of our lives, as if it's our last. When we are able to truly do this—to constantly be in the present and see this moment in all that we are, with no time to shelter hate, keep bitterness in our hearts, or bring hurt and pain to others—every instant of our lives can be appreciated fully, right now, and not tomorrow. Because our tomorrow is not promised.

KEEPING REAL

When I'm asked about the title of my book, *Finding Freedom*, and how I'm able to obtain such a freedom behind the walls of San Quentin—worse still, on death row, and for all the years I have been here—my mind soars above the question and wonders: "Does anybody want to know how badly I want out of prison? Can a practicing Buddhist ever cry foul at the injustice of being here?" Or is the purpose of my being here in prison—no matter rightly or wrongly, justly or unjustly—precisely what lies at the heart of the Buddha's teachings? Freedom can be found in any situation I may be confronted with. True freedom is not about where I am, but rather about the practice of cultivating peace within my heart and mind.

Still, I struggle with the question of what real freedom is. I sit with this question in my daily life. Whenever I hear one of my fellow prisoners say that he will never know true freedom until the day he is finally let out of prison, I wonder if embracing the teachings of the Buddha is just another way I have become institutionalized. Or, does choosing not to wait until I'm out of prison to experience freedom translate into "I'm not trying hard enough to get out of prison"?

How can I, as a Buddhist practitioner on death row, find freedom in myself without being thought foolish by my fellow prisoners or my own mind? How do I answer the self-imposed questions that run rampant in my mind: "What am I doin'? Hell, man...freedom isn't bein' here in prison. Not in prison like this, sittin' on folded blankets on this cold-ass floor and behind this solid door, dude! Freedom is about goin' wherever you please, whenever you want to . . . to the beach . . . the theater . . . being around family and friends again . . ."

In prison, we are left alone with the troubled turbulence of our minds. This agitation either becomes fuel for the prison's towering furnace that belches out bitterness, hatred, and resentment or the mind levitates above our seemingly doomed existence and instead dwells on the real meaning of our lives and the meaning of all life.

From the moment I met my teacher, Chagdud Rinpoche, I wanted to learn how to find some measure of inner peace. I did not try to pronounce the Sanskrit words that I had read in his books, nor did I try to make sense, early on, of their meanings. The scholarly aspects of Buddhism were not for me.

What I remember more than anything else is Rinpoche's emphasis on practice. His words became an echo in my ears: "Practice, and practice, and then do more practice!" I was given the Red Tara practice and meditation, a way of seeing through an open door to states of happiness, inner peace, and ultimate freedom. One sits with the pure nature of the mind that chooses true happiness over suffering and, at the same time, recognizes that no one is free from suffering. It was taking on the bodhisattva vow. I saw how I could compassionately use all my human imperfections, the physical state of my imprisonment, and even the neighbor of the execution chamber, as ways to benefit others. If I could practice in such circumstances, perhaps I could give hope to the hopelessness felt in their lives.

I learned that Buddhist practice was about awakening to the idea that freedom is not obtained by hurrying to get out of prison. Most people aren't in San Quentin, or on death row, and they still do not have the inner peace and freedom that they, like me, desire. I began to recognize my own hurt and pain, and the suffering of all sentient beings. There was no better place to start this spiritual path than where I was. This did not mean, nor does it today, that I don't aspire to get out of prison and not be here one minute longer than I have to. What it does mean is starting where we are. Whenever we start where we are, real freedom is in our practice. Whatever spiritual practice keeps us awake and close to the true nature of our hearts and minds is where freedom can be found.

Often I'm asked by my fellow prisoners what I think freedom is all about. I try not to sound too spiritual. I say, "Freedom is about keeping who you really are real with you." When I am pressed for a more down-to-earth response, I like repeating the words from a song I once heard, "It's about 'freein' your mind and your ass will follow." What I tell myself, almost like a mantra, is that freedom arises out of practice.

The practice of *being*, whether on San Quentin's death row or lying under a favorite tree in the park, leads to real freedom. Real freedom is the practice of cultivating seeds of peace and the time we give to ourselves that affects not only who we are but the whole world around us.

Practicing Buddhism is like being a professional athlete who is rarely seen training even though countless hours have been devoted to working out at the gym. Behind the athlete's "natural" appearance is a commitment to day-to-day, all-year-round practice.

The more practice I do, the more I'm able to feel at peace with myself. And when I watch Tiger Woods skillfully put a golf ball into a tiny hole, or His Holiness the Dalai Lama radiating luminous compassion, I am able to see their practice undisguised. Who they have become is living proof that if I devote myself as strongly toward inner peace, my practice will also bear fruit. And yet, nothing is as easy as it seems.

I remember for years having the vision of "freedom" when I

was allowed outside for exercise time. I would smell the ocean, witness the seagulls gliding overhead, and feel almost extended by my thoughts taking hold of me. I would find myself wishing for the "real freedom" of standing on a beach. feeling the sand between my toes, and watching the waves roll onto the shore. No matter how many times I meditated with the idea that "freedom is right here, where I am now," every exercise day the smell of the salt water caressed my nostrils as I stepped into the early morning fog, and the feeling that I shouldn't be here strangled my heart. Not even walking meditation could loosen its grip. I felt at a loss. I couldn't hear the Buddhist teaching: "Freedom is where you are."

"Yeah, sure," I would mutter. "It's where *you* are, not where I'm at. Give me the ocean, a long walk looking out at the waves . . . not here, in this exercise cage, dodging the droppings of seagulls. Then we'll have a whole lot more in common . . ."

This dialogue with myself continued for several years, until one day I got a card from a friend. Hank was a schoolteacher at one of the most violent inner-city schools in Watts. His letters described the senseless violence of shootings and knifings at his school, the times he had been shot at, and the hopelessness he felt. In some sense, he was a cellmate for me, but in his own prison out in society. We had a lot in common.

I had been encouraging him to give himself a vacation, to get away from that scene for a while. When I got his card with the Hawaii postmark, a smile spread across my face. My friend thanked me for encouraging him to take this vacation. He described lying on a sunny beach where, for the first time in a long time, he was able to finally relax, read a book, and not hear the "rat-tat-tat" of gunshots or the sirens of ambulances chasing by. He ended by wondering if I had ever read *The Silence of the Lambs* by Thomas Harris, the book he was reading.

I was in disbelief. I had not read the book but I had seen the movie. It was gruesome. A prison favorite. I couldn't believe Hank had traveled all those thousands of miles to lie on a sunny beach, to get away from all the violence, only to be reading about a ruthless psychopath.

It was then that I realized, almost like a slap across the back of my head by the Buddha himself, that being on a beach, any beach, could not make me any more or less free; that real freedom is about the practice of being. Whether we are on a sunny beach or inside the concrete walls of a prison, real freedom comes from realizing how the true nature of our minds is like an empty field. The seeds we plant, and constantly nurture and cultivate, will eventually give us the sense of being at home with our hearts, no matter where we are.

This has been so true for me. When I'm asked how I'm able to find freedom behind the walls of San Quentin's death row, I still wonder, "Does anybody want to know how badly I want out of prison?" Being asked the question is encouraging to me. It is an indication that my practice has allowed me to manifest some sense of peace, of freedom. Their asking is also a reminder that real freedom is no easier to find outside these prison walls than inside them. I'm helped by this fact. Whenever I meditate, I know that others in sanghas all over the world are seated next to me.

EPILOGUE

I began to write stories about my life so I could look into it, understand it more fully. My writing and spiritual practice have become inseparable.

It is almost unimaginable to think of what I might be like if I didn't have the dharma, my teacher, Chagdud Tulku Rinpoche, and the love and care of my friends. They have enabled me to turn a situation as bad as mine into an opportunity to be of some benefit, if not for myself, then for school kids and their teachers and counselors who write to say that I'm making a difference, that my writings and my example are an inspiration in their lives. I hope to be able to continue, because it allows me to transcend my present circumstances, to transform everything around me into something almost radiant, filled with a chance to make a difference in my own life and in the world.

The freedom to be and express myself is what's most important to me. It means waking up every morning, content with the dharma in my life, with my prayers to be of benefit to others, and with my writings giving voice to my human worth. I simply want to live day by day as close to all my aspirations and freedom as I can.

I want to leave my writing behind for when I am gone and the question of who I was enters people's minds. If I am executed, there will be some who believe I deserved it. But those who want to try to make sense of it will see, through my writing, a human being who made mistakes. Maybe my writing will at least help them see me as someone who felt, loved, and cared, someone who wanted to know for himself who he was. My writing will hopefully show those people that they could easily have been me.

AFTERWORD TO THE 2020 EDITION

When I was invited to write a new afterword to this new edition of *Finding Freedom*, I began to think of all the Pablos and Bryans, and of Joe Bob and Pete—the scars on their bare skin shining under the hot sun that day on the prison exercise yard.

It's now more than twenty years later. Where are those guys? Where would any one of us be—two decades later?

To think of where I would be if I had never been in San Quentin State Prison to write *Finding Freedom* is easy: I would be dead. I would have wasted away in the early years of my life—most likely by the violence that I found myself in, that circle of friends I thought I wanted and that I had to have. We would've had no homes to go to. We would group up in the recreation field at Juvie and tattoo our bodies with gang turf images, once inside, with the older boys at State Youth Authorities. Then, eventually one day—if we made it that far—scarred in waist chains and leg irons, one by one in single file, escorted into hardened cell blocks in the infamous North and South Wing housing units at San Quentin.

It's fortunate that I'm alive. And over time, becoming a practicing Buddhist, I have seen these doors open many hearts.

I have been blessed to receive thousands of letters from all walks of life that inspire me—from grade schools to colleges, to the sons and daughters of prison guards, to prisoners still in or still out—and all to say, "If you can do it in a place like San Quentin, I could here on the outside."

Over the years, they have given me both joys and tears—the affirmation of my humanity, admittedly, in times of depression and despair.

Many people have asked me why I did not go into the details of the case that landed me on death row in the first edition of my book. At the time, I was simply trying to survive this place. To find some ground beneath my feet. I trust the truth of my innocence to find its way.

It is my hope that *Finding Freedom* goes on to help us find the best in ourselves. It is with my heartfelt prayer that it will continue to be of benefit to all beings.

JARVIS JAY MASTERS
East Block—San Quentin
March 2020

AFTERWORD

by H.E. Chagdud Tulku Rinpoche

All of us live in a prison called *samsara*, cyclic existence, and not one of us is free from suffering. In addition to distress experienced in the course of birth, old age, sickness, and death, we find ourselves in situations of anguish, prison, war, famine, abuse, grief, and acute frustration of our needs and desires. To find release, we must first recognize the source of our pain.

Nothing is accomplished by blaming God, or parents, or the police, or outer enemies. The source of suffering is karma ripening from seeds we have planted in the long-forgotten past, including previous lifetimes. Whatever actions we took based on virtue—kindness, compassion, and love—are the cause of the happiness we experience now. And vice versa, the pain and negative conditions we experience have arisen from selfishness and anger and ignorance of what to accept and what to reject. Few people should trust their past karma. Rich, dynamic, good-looking people can experience shocking reversals of fortune, including violent attacks, accidents, sickness, and other causes of ruin. "What an unbelievable tragedy!" we exclaim, not realizing that it is an inevitable outcome of unrecognized, unpurified karma.

To acknowledge our own karma as the cause of our experience empowers us to purify it and transform our future. To understand that we are not unique in our suffering, to look for a way to reduce suffering for ourselves and others, gives birth to authentic compassion, beyond mere pity. In this book, Jarvis Masters demonstrates taking these steps and entering the path toward liberation. Against great odds, he has made the commitment to refrain from harsh responses and harmful actions. He has found the basic goodness of his own true nature and extended his intention to benefit others. Ultimately, compassion and beneficial intention must become impartial and include both victim and aggressor. If we contemplate deeply, we may even develop more compassion for the aggressor because, while the moment of suffering purifies the victim's karma, in the same moment the aggressor is creating the causes that give rise to cycle after cycle of hellish pain in the future.

We need not wait passively until our nonvirtuous karma flares into unfortunate circumstances before we purify it. We can invoke as our witness an enlightened presence—God, Jesus, Buddha—whomever we recognize as the embodiment of supreme compassion, omniscience, and power. We acknowledge our negative actions of body, speech, and mind—actions remembered or not, actions in this and former lifetimes. Surely some negativity remains or we would now be enlightened wisdom beings ourselves, devoid of anger and selfish desires. We then make the commitment not to repeat such actions and visualize that, from our spiritual witness, radiant light or purifying nectar arises, completely pervading us and cleansing our nonvirtuous karma.

When past harmfulness has already ripened into difficult situations, we can still use this meditation to purify it. And if, during a painful period, we can transcend self-focus for even one instant with the thought, "May my own suffering prevent others from having to experience this," the power of our compassion will purify immense amounts of negative karma and the power of our good heart will guarantee more pleasurable circumstances in the future.

May such happiness arise for Jarvis and for all who read his book. Ultimately, may all beings be released from the endless cycles of karmic delusion and find liberation into a state of enlightenment.

H.E. CHAGDUD TULKU RINPOCHE (1930–2002) was a Tibetan Buddhist meditation master and the author of three books: *Gates to Buddhist Practice, Lord of the Dance,* and *Life in Relation to Death.*

ABOUT THE AUTHOR

Jarvis Jay Masters was born in Long Beach, California, in 1962. He is a widely published African American Buddhist writer and the author of *That Bird Has My Wings: The Autobiography of an Innocent Man on Death Row*. His poem "Recipe for Prison Pruno" won the PEN Award in 1992. He has kept an active correspondence with teachers and students across the country for two decades, and his work continues to be studied in classrooms in both grade schools and colleges. In collaboration with the Truthworkers, a hip-hop theatre company for youth in New York City dedicated to issues of social justice, his work has been adapted and performed in a variety of venues including the National Cathedral and Lincoln Center for the Performing Arts.

Since taking formal refuge vows with H.E. Chagdud Tulku Rinpoche in 1991, Jarvis has also been guided by Ven. Pema Chödrön, with whom he shares an enduring friendship. In 2020, he became the subject of a podcast series *Dear Governor* as well as a new biography, *The Buddhist on Death Row: How One Man Found Light in the Darkest Place*, by David Sheff.

Originally sent to San Quentin State Prison in 1981 for armed robbery, Jarvis was convicted of conspiracy to murder a prison guard in 1985 and sentenced to death in 1990. Because his case involved a correctional officer, he was placed in solitary confinement and endured there for twenty-one years, from 1985 to 2007. Jarvis exhausted his state appeals in 2019, and his case is currently headed to the federal courts. For more information on the growing campaign to exonerate him, go to www.freejarvis.org.

Portions of this book have previously appeared in a different form in the following anthologies and publications: *Brotherman: The Odyssey of Black Men in America—An Anthology*, edited by Herb Boyd and Robert L. Allen; *Where the Heart Is: A Celebration of Home*, edited by Julienne Bennett and Mimi Luebbermann; *The Awakened Warrior: Living with Courage, Compassion, and Discipline*, edited by Rick Fields; *Turning Wheel: Journal of the Buddhist Peace Fellowship*; *Utne Reader*; *Wingspan: Journal of the Male Spirit*; *Men's Studies Review: A Publication of the Men's Studies Association*; *Recovering: The Adventure of Life Beyond Addiction*; *North Coast Xpress*; *ReSource: Changes Magazine*; *Endeavor*; *Body Memories: Radical Perspectives of Childhood Sexual Abuse*; *Inquiring Mind*; *Prison Writing*. "Mourning Exercise" has been reprinted here courtesy of the *San Francisco Chronicle*, where it appeared on April 14, 1996.

LIBRARY OF CONGRESS CATALOGING-IN-PUBLICATION DATA

Names: Masters, Jarvis Jay, 1962– author. | Chödrön, Pema, writer of foreword.
Title: Finding freedom: how death row broke and opened my heart / Jarvis Jay Masters; foreword by Pema Chödrön.
Description: Boulder, Colorado: Shambhala, 2020.
Identifiers: LCCN 2020008932 |
ISBN 9781611809114 (trade paperback)
Subjects: LCSH: Prisoners' writings, American—California— San Quentin. | Death row inmates—Literary collections. | Prisoners—Literary collections. | Prisons—Literary collections.
Classification: LCC PS3563.A826 F56 2020 |
DDC 810.8/0920692—dc23
LC record available at https://lccn.loc.gov/2020008932